Staircase C

STAIRCASE C

Elvire Murail

Translated by M. L. Linden

C

CENTURY PUBLISHING
LONDON

First published in Great Britain in 1986 by
Century Hutchinson Ltd
Brookmount House, 62–65 Chandos Place
London WC2N 4NW

Published by arrangement with Sylvie Messinger, Paris

ISBN 0 7126 9406 4

Printed in Great Britain by
St Edmundsbury Press, Bury St Edmunds, Suffolk
Bound by Butler & Tanner Ltd, Frome, Somerset

"Inheritor of more than earth can
Give"
—Percy Bysshe Shelley

1. *We'll no more to the woods*

I gave up going to the innocent woods of childhood the day I discovered that I preferred Bosch's *Garden of Earthly Delights* to Renoir's *Little Girl with a Watering Can.* That's not simply a metaphor. Through my work as an art critic—now there's a profession!—I had lost all spontaneity and all inclination toward things fresh and new. Besides, it's easier to talk of horror, in all its beauty, than of happiness. While I wandered about in the *Garden of Earthly Delights,* my innocence had gone astray. And in choosing gardens over the woods, I was becoming truly insufferable.

That's when I decided on a trip to the country—to remind me of childhood and nursery rhymes. Remote as my relatively humble dwelling in Greenwich Village may be from the towering midtown skyscrapers or the doormen and limousines of Park Avenue, it is still far from pastoral. Short on ideas, I thought I'd ask the advice of my upstairs neighbor, Colin Shepherd. Though I hadn't known Colin for long, his persistent habit of letting his bathtub run over had me often going up to rail at him.

Before leaving my apartment, I paused to admire myself in the bathroom mirror: a man in his early thirties, a well-built, handsome lad. I do consider myself good-looking, thanks. It's my right.

When I reached the fourth floor and rang Colin Shepherd's door bell, he couldn't be disturbed. Obviously in a bad mood, he shut the door in my face, saying he didn't give a shit about my problems. Just then, Bruce Conway, another tenant, appeared. He was on his way downstairs, jumping the steps with both feet together.

"Another domestic crisis?" He threw me a lopsided grin. "If Col Shepherd won't have anything to do with you, just come to my place. I'll give you some jasmine tea."

When I explained my problem, Bruce replied that he couldn't imagine what I might possibly find exciting about the country.

"That's just it," I told him. "I don't want to do anything exciting. I want to be bored to death. No movies, no hot-dog stands, and, above all, no art critics. I want some dismal spot where there are nothing but trees, flowers, and little birds."

Again Bruce gave me his lopsided smile, his specialty, and with blue eyes raised to the ceiling, he began to rock back and forth on his running shoes.

"Hey, mister, what are li'l boids?" he asked.

"They're like buses, without the passengers."

He rewarded me with a thwack on the back and a laugh. Bruce spends a good part of his time jostling me.

"That's not bad! I'll quote you."

"Copyright Foster Tuncurry, all rights reserved, USSR included."

Bruce shifted his stance. Leaning against the stair rail, he began to hop from one foot to the other on the first step. I was waiting for him to bust his skull.

Two floors down, a door slammed violently. Both of us peered over the railing. Virgil Sparks had just left Beatrice Holt's apartment after a shouting match, or so it appeared. As Virgil started up the stairs toward his own apartment right across from mine, Bruce couldn't resist reeling off a bit of Dante.

"Lasciate ogni speranza, voi ch'entrate. . . But why is Virgil so determined to break past the gates of Hades?"

"Get your ass down here if you're man enough!" Virgil hollered.

"Why don't you haul your ass up here!"

"You want to say that again?"

"Come on up, asshole! Now that I've said it again, just come ahead!"

"Oh, fuck off, Conway. I'm really in no mood to fool around."

I knew Virgil Sparks very well. He worked for the same jerk-off I did (read: "our most honorable editor-in-chief"). A good journalist, he was dead set on being a writer, always wrangling about his articles with Macland. Not I. Macland accepted my pieces without comment because they were "cultural." So he had nothing to argue about, aside from goading me occasionally with phrases such as, "Does that dabbler really think he'll get someplace with those grease stains on canvas?"

Anyway, Macland was wasting his time, because I rarely answered his outbursts. But he handled Virgil differently. He addressed him only as Mr. Virgil Bentley Sparks, thereby mocking Virgil's insistence that his whole name be inscribed at the end of his articles. Virgil wrote under the headings of "film" and "theatre," areas Macland unfortunately believed he knew well.

But Virgil's true passion was called Beatrice Holt. She had been living in a one-bedroom apartment on the second floor for three years, about the time I, too, moved into Stairway C. In fact, the super had given me wrong information, and I thought my apartment was to be on the second floor. That's how Beatrice and I happened to meet in front of the same door. The error was quickly corrected, and she invited me in to see her apartment. Then we went up to mine to compare the two. On the stairs we passed Virgil, who looked at me with surprised recognition.

"But you're Foster Tuncurry!" he exclaimed.

I stared at him anxiously, trying desperately to figure out who he was. But this tall young man with brown hair merely stood there, blushing and helping me not one bit. In my line of work I'm obliged to talk to too many people at too many cocktail parties. More than once I've been confronted with terrifying individuals who recount our last conversation in detail, including what I was wearing, that I had a cold, and asking to be remembered to so-and-so, of whom I have not the slightest recollection, either.

"Well, hello. How are—" I began cautiously.

"Virgil Bentley Sparks," he leaped in spontaneously.

I breathed a sigh of relief.

"Yes, of course. How funny that we should wind up in the same building."

Already Virgil had totally lost interest in me. Scarlet in the face, he was staring at Beatrice.

"Your wife, no doubt?" he choked out with some difficulty.

"Good God, no!" I blurted.

"Well, thanks a lot," Beatrice spat.

"I only meant," I said by way of apology, "that I have no intention of marrying anyone, not even you, oh Goddess of the Second Floor. Mr. Sparks, Miss Holt—she's your new neighbor too. Just your day!"

Virgil relaxed, recognizing that he wouldn't have to cross my dead body for access to the young woman. At the time Beatrice had long brown hair. One day she had it cut off in a fit of rage, and since then, she's been a redhead. Though small in stature, she radiates enough energy and force to rock even the most confident display of machismo. So it didn't take her more than one gulp to gobble up that yellow canary, Virgil Sparks. (I don't know why, but Virgil has always put me in mind of a canary.)

Since that day, Beatrice and Virgil have been Stairway C's most avidly followed item. Each and every day doors fly open as shrieks begin to echo through the stairwell. From one landing to the next, comments fly back and forth on the insults and injuries clearly emitted by our pair of lovers.

If there's a good retort, we applaud, and at the final curtain we declare the evening's winner. This is no cruel game on our part, for there is no way to take Beatrice's fury and Virgil's wailing seriously. It's simply that some individuals cannot manage to love each other except in five-act tragedies and six-volume sagas. One gets inured to it. But let's get back to that day when Virgil challenged Bruce Conway.

"Me? Fuck off?" replied the unbearable Bruce. "But I have a reputation to uphold, sir!" Bruce was taking great delight in all of this.

Wearing an evil expression, Virgil quickly reached our landing. "What are the two of you doing in front of Shepherd's door?"

"We're lining up," I said. "To take a bath."

They laughed, well aware of my altercations with Colin Shepherd on the subject of his incontinent bathtub.

"How about a drink?" suggested Bruce.

"Good idea. We'll go up to your place," I declared.

"Why my place?"

"Because it was your idea and because you have the best vodka in the whole house."

"Well, at the moment I'm all out."

"No matter. You also have the best bourbon in the house."

So we went up one flight, and while Bruce was putting his key in the lock, Colin's door opened. I leaned over the railing and watched him set his numerous locks.

"You haven't left any taps running, I hope," I sang down at him.

Raising his head, he clapped a hand to his mouth, and his green eyes opened wide.

"Oh, wow! Lucky you mentioned it!"

As he turned back to undo all the locks again, I began to laugh. He ran into the apartment, and I could hear him swear.

Virgil sneered. "Think he really forgot to turn off the water?"

Soon Colin came out again, whistling.

"So?" I asked.

"Oh, nothing," he answered. "I just unplugged the toaster."

"That's all?"

"Well, it sticks, and there was some bread in it."

"One day you're going to blow us all up, you and your empty head!" I turned to Virgil. "Really, there are times I'd like to belt him one! Don't let me do it, Virg."

"I bet he'd just love that."

Though Bruce had spoken softly, Colin heard and looked up at us.

"You're a bastard, Bruce Conway!"

"It wasn't intended unkindly," I answered.

Bruce bit his lower lip. Then he leaned perilously far out over the balustrade to make amends. "You know I never miss a chance to put my foot in it, Shep."

"So it appears," mumbled Colin as he went on downstairs. "Never."

Colin was the last to move into Stairway C, about a year ago. Actually, at the time he wasn't alone. He was playing flunky to a brute who called himself Hal. Colin had already been working as a dress designer for a year or two, and to all appearances, it was he who had the money.

Taller than his victim by several inches, Hal was certainly the sole creature in the whole place I had no wish to talk to.

None of us had any contact with them during the first three months, and we'd all scrupulously avoided the fourth floor.

Then, one night, I was coming home with Suzy—my girlfriend at the time, though I dropped her the day Bruce told me she looked dumb, and I abruptly realized that it was not appearances alone. Well, that night, as we were merrily making our way to my bachelor quarters, we passed Colin, who was hurtling down the stairs. He had a gash in his brow, and blood was coursing down his face and onto his shirt. I stopped him in midflight and asked if he needed help.

"There's n-nothing you can do for me," he stammered.

"Colin!"

Hal's voice echoed down the stairwell. Under my hand Colin Shepherd's arm turned to gooseflesh.

"Colin! Come back here immediately!"

The wretched boy started up the stairs with an expression of so much sadness and pain that I turned to follow him.

"No," he said softly. "There's nothing you can do for me."

The next day in Virgil's apartment, I asked Bruce and Virgil what they made of it.

"After all, we really can't let the poor kid be skinned alive and not raise a finger," I insisted when I understood that they weren't anxious to get mixed up in the thing.

"Frankly, Foster, their problems are absolutely none of our business," answered Virgil with a shrug.

"But come on!" I shouted. "If a man were beating his wife to the point of splitting her skull, you'd get high and mighty about demanding justice! Because Colin is gay, you undoubtedly believe that this is just part of his perversion."

"But he himself refused your offer of help!"

"So! A lot of women don't complain or admit that they've been beaten. Shepherd is weak; he's scared of that gorilla, that's all."

At that point Beatrice showed up, letting herself into Virgil's apartment with a duplicate set of keys. And she gave me a kind look of approval.

"Good for you, Foster!" she said. "I like that attitude. As for you two, you're nothing but insensitive cads. When I passed the poor guy this morning, I was ashamed. Totally! For three months now we've been voluntarily ignoring the doings of that goon who's treating a sweet, gentle guy like his slave! It's revolting."

Virgil blushed faintly, his eyes firmly fixed on his coffee cup. He finally agreed. "But what do you want to do about it?"

"The best way would be to talk to Colin himself," I suggested. "To convince him that he shouldn't let himself be intimidated by that son of a bitch."

"Splendid idea, Foster, and lots of luck!" Bruce shot at me as he got up.

I sighed with resignation.

"Okay, damn it! I will talk to him."

That very afternoon I ran into Colin at the local supermarket. He was buying a can of peas. I smiled, pointing a thumb at the can. "I loathe green peas!"

"Me too," he said, making an effort to smile back.

I grabbed the opportunity.

"Then don't buy them!"

"But—"

"Who's going to eat them if you don't?"

"Oh, I'll eat them all right. Hal says—"

"Shep, listen: send that guy packing! I wish you understood that if you want to, you can kick him out! If need be, you could ask us to help. And I assure you that if you kick him out with conviction, he won't come back."

"But—"

"No buts. It's for your own good, for your health, your life, even."

"But . . . I love him," he replied with disarming simplicity.

"And what about him, does he love you?"

"No."

"Come on then, be reasonable! If you at least put up a little resistance, he wouldn't beat you anymore."

"But it's just because I do resist that he hits me."

I was beginning to run short of ideas. The problem was delicate in the extreme.

"Well, at any rate, if you need us someday, please don't hesitate to call for help."

"Thanks."

I left, quite disappointed and anxious. As I turned to look back before going through the checkout, however, I noticed that he had put the can back on the shelf. I made a report to Beatrice, whom I met coming out of the corner bar.

"Looking for Virgil again?" I asked.

Showing me a pack of cigarettes, she burst out laughing.

"No, it's for me! I came down to buy some cigarettes."

I told her about my failure with Colin.

She sighed, nodding. "We can only cross our fingers. What a pity! Such a gorgeous guy too!"

"I'm available!"

"But not as handsome."

"Thanks a bunch. That's always great to hear."

"Anyway, you've got a nasty misogynist streak. Frankly you're no bargain. Are you unaware of it, or do you do it on purpose?"

"Do what?"

"Treat women like . . . like something disposable. A good cigar! Women are no more important to you than that!"

"They've never complained," I retorted.

"Well, take a look at the girls you date!"

"Hey, what is this? Who put you on the judge's bench? And how about you? After all, you're not married to Virgil, and I have it on reliable authority that you do more than hold hands and gaze into one another's eyes!"

"What reliable authority?"

"Your own, idiot! Don't you remember?"

"Foster, you know damn well I'm no reliable authority. When's the last time you caught me telling the truth?"

On my way home I passed the sixth-floor tenant, Mrs. Bernhardt. I knew almost nothing about her. She wasn't really part of the Stairway C family. Or you could say she played the role of the great-grandmother nobody notices until the day she dies, leaving an indefinable void. Mrs. Bernhardt moved in here after the death of her husband, a black man who also happened to be Jewish. I was totally ignorant about her life, her work, whether she had children or whatever. . . . Sad to say, I didn't really care.

"Hello, Mrs. Bernhardt," I said in an effort to be nice.

"Hello, Mr. Tuncurry."

Quickly turning away, she went back to her halting ascent,

for she had trouble walking. Her crumpled face, black as a prune, never displayed a smile.

That evening I was fuming over the text of my article on Hieronymus Bosch when a terrible scream came down from the fourth floor. I dashed out, just as Virgil flung open his door across the hall. Our eyes met.

"This time no one can tell me he isn't being throttled!" I exclaimed.

In front of Colin's door we met up with Bruce Conway. "What'll we do?" he asked. "Now you can't hear a thing."

"Let's ring," I answered. "Then we'll see." I pressed the door bell.

"Who's there?" said a voice I recognized as Hal's.

"Your neighbors. We'd like to talk to Colin."

"He's not here."

"The hell he isn't!" said Bruce. "Open up right away, or we're calling the cops."

"By what right?"

"By the right of a full night's sleep."

"Get lost."

"The hell we will!" Bruce flared. He cast us a warning look. "God damn it, I'm breaking down the door. Stand back, you guys!"

I was surprised to see that beneath a rather nonchalant and ungainly exterior, Bruce concealed an uncommon agility and a good set of muscles. It took three tries before he broke through the wood around the handle and locks. When we first got through, we couldn't see anyone. Hal had taken refuge in a bedroom with his pistol.

"Don't come nearer or I'll shoot!" he warned.

Bruce stepped forward and burst out laughing. "If you want to get us, you'd better use something besides that thing!"

Hal studied him, unsure. Discovering a new hatred for that brute face, I staunchly moved in closer. Hal watched me without moving, still not budging as I took the weapon from his hands.

"Where's Colin?" I asked him roughly.

"In the bathroom," he mumbled.

Bruce opened the door beside him. Inside, Colin's body was bathed in a mixture of bathtub water and his own blood. Virgil paled at the sight, and I thought he was about to crumple.

"You watch Hal," I ordered, shoving him back.

"He isn't dead!" Bruce cried out. "Help me get him out!"

I pulled the drain plug, as the pink water was getting to me. Then I grabbed Colin's legs while Bruce lifted his shoulders. Virgil, standing in the doorway, pointed to a kitchen knife in the basin.

As far as we could guess, Hal must have entertained himself by slashing his victim's arms and chest. Why had he dunked Colin in the cold water? we wondered. To revive him?

All three of us stood there, horribly fascinated, when the sound of running feet aroused us abruptly. Hal had just taken off, and we were never to see him again.

This was the first and last time Bruce Conway acted like a reasonable adult. He called the police, the fire department, a doctor, and God knows who else; then he set up watches at Colin's bedside. The body wounds, though numerous, were not really serious. As for the wound to Colin's esteem, that was certainly slow to heal.

Which brings us back to the moment when Bruce Conway, from the fifth floor, delivered his ridiculous observation to Colin Shepherd below.

"Really, Bruce," Virgil sermonized, "you could pay some attention to what you say!"

"It simply slipped out. But what Foster said about belting him—that wasn't so great, either," he added with a jab of the elbow to my ribs. "I'm not the only one to put his foot in his mouth."

"No, but in your case it's chronic," I retorted. "Okay, so how about that drink?"

"Thinks of nothing but drink, this guy," grumbled Bruce, giving me a shove into his two-room apartment.

As I've already mentioned, one of Bruce's characteristics is this habit of always jabbing me. Like a kid of five trying to punch his father. Yet Bruce is well beyond that age. In fact, he's older than I am.

He had been living on the fifth floor for four years or so. The first evidence of his existence came from his cat. When I found the unprepossessing animal on my doorstep, I immediately fell for him. Minus one eye and with ears swollen from countless scraps with his cohorts, he won me over on the spot. I ventured to pat his fur, which was black and dirty—actually quite rare in

a cat—and got in return a swipe of his paw, which left three
lovely streaks of blood on my hand. I whacked him and tried to
get through my door. He followed me in, snarling, while I
cursed at him. Once settled down on my sofa, nothing would
persuade him to leave. In desperation I asked Virgil who might
own this scavenger of garbage cans. To my great surprise he
immediately recognized him.

"That's Bruce Conway's monster."

"And who is Bruce Conway?"

"He's on five, and he's in-sup-*por*-ta-ble!"

From his affectionate tone I took it that Virgil had a great
weakness for Bruce.

"What can I do? The creature won't leave my sofa."

"You could try a bucket of water."

"And ruin everything? No, I'll go see your friend Bruce and
ask him to reclaim his animal."

That's how I met Bruce and Agamemnon. Bruce had to make
use of a broom in order to get his charming little companion out
of my place. Since then, Agamemnon and I have dwelt in perfect harmony. Nothing and nobody can prevent him from coming in here, from ransacking my kitchen from top to bottom and
flexing his claws on my furniture. Strangely I feel an extreme
sympathy toward him, and I remain the sole human authorized
to hold him on my lap. Mysteries abound.

"What's the matter with Beatrice this time?" asked Bruce as
he poured bourbon into the glasses.

Raising his eyes to the ceiling, Virgil grumbled something
like, "Always the same runaround."

"Apropos of that," Bruce went on, "Foster here is planning
to go to the country. You wouldn't have any ideas, would
you?"

"What do you mean, 'apropos of that'?"

"Oh, nothing in particular. Anyway, I thought that you
might benefit from a change of scenery too."

"The country . . . what an odd idea." Virgil was looking at
me with surprise.

"Well, what I mean is . . . I really need it," I replied.
"Sometimes I feel overwhelmed."

"That's because you're alone," said Virgil, lighting up like
a Christmas tree. "What you need is a woman."

Bruce broke into laughter and gave me a slap on the thigh. "Hear that? Pretty funny, eh?"

"I don't see what's so comical." Virgil studied Bruce with contempt. "It's altogether sensible. Love's all that counts."

"Oh, sure! Quite clear where love gets you!"

"But I'm perfectly happy," Virgil said, defending himself.

"That's not the problem," I cut in. "Women I have, thank you very much."

"Women perhaps, but not *a* woman. Therein lies the difference, my poor friend. You simply do not know love."

"First of all, I'm not your poor friend," I retorted with irritation. "And second, you know nothing about my private life or state of mind."

"No, but we do know what you bring home!" roared Bruce, seeming mightily amused. "You can hardly call that women!"

Virgil and Bruce doubled up with laughter, to which I could only respond with glacial disdain.

"I cannot understand what's gotten into you," I said. "I'm not asking your views on my conquests. I'd like some ideas about places to go."

"Conquests!" Bruce roared with a kick of the elbow, which resulted in a partly spilled whiskey.

I got rid of the other half by throwing it in Bruce's grinning face.

"Such good whiskey!" he protested as I stood up to leave.

"We have nothing more to say to each other," I threw back over my shoulder. "I have better things to do than listen to the demented laughter of two idiots."

As I slammed the door, Virgil and Bruce collapsed in renewed hilarity. On my way downstairs I passed Josh Hardy, the second tenant on the sixth floor, Mrs. Bernhardt's neighbor. A man of about fifty-five and divorced for some time, he's a seven-year resident of Stairway C.

Josh's principal characteristic is clear the moment one sees his nose: he is an alcoholic. To my eyes he is extremely sympathetic, perhaps because there is a rather fascinating penniless-bum aspect to him. He works at a nearby printing press where they keep him on no matter what, since he is an excellent typographer.

"Greetings!" he said cheerfully, emitting a whiff of the grape.

"Greetings, disciple of Bacchus!" I replied with a smile.

"The master of us all, sages of the world," he added with the same good humor.

We each went our way. Somewhat saddened, I let myself into my apartment. I felt as if a whole day had been wasted. I still had no idea where to go on vacation—and the taunts of Bruce and Virgil had deeply disturbed me. Disturbed not because they were unkind but because they were full of truth. I opened the morning mail, neglected until that moment, finding there an invitation to an art exhibition followed by refreshments.

Sighing at the prospect of a cocktail party, I suddenly noticed that the opening was to be the next day. Once again a publicity department seemed to have gone about their work the wrong way. Who would dare send out invitations this late? I could very well avoid going on the pretext of not having received word in time. But I also figured I could corner the publicist there and complain—one way to vent my frustrations over the misery and boredom that were shaping my life.

2. *In which the day begins with scones and ends with tripe*

At nine o'clock the next morning, I cast aside with a groan the book I'd been reading in bed. Colin Shepherd had just put on *The Rite of Spring* at top volume. I gave up the idea of banging on the ceiling in favor of going upstairs. Colin opened the door and, on seeing me, allowed a broad grin to spread across his naughty-cherub face.

"Oh, hello."

"Say, listen, do you suppose you could spare your speakers the agony?"

I regretted my sharp tone the moment I saw his smile fade.

"Sure. I'm sorry."

"It's not that I don't like Stravinsky, but too much is too much."

"I'm constantly blundering, I guess."

"You said it!"

"You know, I've been thinking . . . well, maybe it would be wise for me to leave a set of keys with one of you, in case I went out without turning off the stove."

"You're right, that would be a splendid idea."

Crossing the living room, Colin quickly opened a drawer, took out his duplicate keys, and held them out to me.

"Here."

Only then, as I stepped into the room to take the keys, did dawn on me that Colin wasn't wearing a shirt. I reached out a hand toward his and took the bunch of keys. Somewhat befuddled by the loud music and the shock of seeing Colin's naked chest, I didn't budge as I watched him close the door.

20

"Like a cup of coffee?" he asked, turning down the volume on his stereo.

"No, I've just had some."

I was feeling increasingly ill at ease, with strange ideas drifting through my head. Here I was closed up all alone with this nut—and with probably not another soul in the building. Even if I called for help . . . After all, this guy had submitted to the torture of a sadist. Perhaps he was perverted in other ways. . . .

I had begun to think of an excuse for escape when Colin said innocently, "I've just made some scones. You want some?"

Oh, what the hell! "With raisins?" I couldn't help asking.

"Naturally, with raisins."

He disappeared into the kitchen, and I sat down on his sofa, inwardly railing at myself. Had I been Christ in the desert and the devil had tempted me with scones, I would have succumbed. Fortunately a rather remote likelihood, all in all. . . . Colin returned with a heavily laden tray, and once more I felt queasy at the sight of the fine white scars crisscrossing his torso.

"Don't you feel cold?" I asked sharply.

Colin's eyes widened with sudden understanding.

"Oh, yes . . . in fact, I was just getting dressed when you rang."

He vanished into his bedroom, and I sighed with relief. My eyes rested on the low table at the hodgepodge: coffeepot, two cups, a plateful of scones, butter, orange marmalade, two spoons, a knife, and the sugar bowl. I chose my scone with care, split it open, and buttered it with intense pleasure. It was still warm, crisp on the outside and soft at the center. My taste buds quivered in ecstasy at the first taste of the butter. Real butter, not margarine.

I was reaching toward the plate again when Colin came back in, wearing a checked shirt open halfway to his belt. After flipping the record he sat down facing me, cross-legged on the floor. The music started up again, and Colin poured coffee into the two cups. Pushing one toward me, he helped himself to two lumps of sugar. Then he looked me over with the trace of a smile and reached for a scone.

"There's some marmalade too," he said.

"No, I prefer butter."

"Yes, me too. How many lumps do you take?"

"Just one, thanks."

I stirred the coffee absently while I ate.

"Well, then, they're good?"

"Super. Never tasted better."

"I'm pretty good at cooking in general, but I have a few specialties—scones, sherbets, glazed pork ribs, braised beef."

"Braised beef?"

"Yes, French-style, of course."

"I have fond memories of braised beef. When I was a kid, I went everywhere with my parents. My father was in the diplomatic service, and we lived in France for fifteen years. Now they've settled in Switzerland." I hesitated an instant before adding, "And yours?"

"Mine?" Colin laughed. "They're totally uninteresting."

I firmly changed the subject. "You're not working this morning?"

"No. In my racket you can stay home if you've gotten the job done in time. Would you like to see? I have a couple of sketches on my drawing board."

He got to his feet without using his hands, a demonstration of pliancy that reminded me of my high-school gymnastic classes. He showed me his sketches: women in bathing suits with hats on. Colin apologized for their lack of interest, but it was sort of an assignment.

"They're terrific," I said. "You never draw for your own pleasure? Landscapes, portraits, stuff?"

"Yeah, I do stuff. Stuff, above all else, it so happens."

"Yes, well . . . you know what I mean."

"You want to see my stuff?"

"Sure. If it's no trouble."

Very carefully Colin drew from a large portfolio three sheets, which he laid out on the floor. Straightening up a bit to see them, I caught my breath. I left the sofa and got down on my knees in front of the sheets.

"I do it in ink. Natural India inks. They're three panels of one work. There are others to come."

I wasn't trying to understand what was represented. They seemed a hybrid of prints and illuminations. On the first I made out a sort of ladder.

"It's Jacob's ladder?" I asked, very softly in fear of dispelling the magic of the inks.

"No, it's Stairway C."

I gave a start.

"It's a triptych of Stairway C," Colin added, crouching down beside me. "After this I'll do the whole house, then the street, the neighborhood. And then all of Manhattan."

"It's really beautiful."

"Would you like me to explain it?"

"No! Most certainly not."

"You really find it beautiful?"

"It's astonishing. Are you planning a show?"

"And you'd come to do articles on me? No, thanks!"

"Do you have any others?"

Colin hesitated a moment before saying, "Yes, but I don't want to show them to you."

"Very good. That proves there's an artist in you."

He blushed faintly, wavering.

"Don't make fun of me."

"I'm not making fun of you. Never in my life have I seen anything like this. These are the mailboxes?"

"Yes."

As tiny details in all directions gradually took on meaning for me, I couldn't help laughing. Lying flat on my stomach for a better view of the sketches, I forgot about everything including the scones.

"Bruce's cat!" I cried out when I discovered it in the second drawing. "And this here . . . it's your bathtub?"

I was bursting with pleasure at each new invention of Colin's creative delirium. I saw that the tub figured in the first and third drawings. In this last a line stood for the floor (that is, my ceiling), and underneath was reproduced in miniature the kitsch light fixture that graced my bathroom. Oddly, it was painted in red even though its true color is blue. I was on the verge of asking the reason for this when I noticed that both the ceiling and the bottom of his bathtub were red also. It was quite clear. In the same image Colin had depicted a tub filled with blood and one that was running over. I trembled.

"That's my bathtub," said Colin, still crouching beside me.

I could feel his eyes on my shoulders, and their weight was such that I had to look his way.

"What's bothering you?" he asked.

"Nothing."

"Oh, yes, there is. What is it? That I let some guy torture

me? Or that I'm gay? What do you know about me? Do you know one single thing about my desires or my pleasures? Why are you embarrassed? You think I'm going to jump on you? The first thing you learn when you're gay is that most other people aren't, that they're free to choose. That's why you have nothing to fear. I've never forced myself on anyone. I'm neither crazy nor dangerous nor perverted. Just condemned for life. Like Mrs. Bernhardt.''

"Mrs. Bernhardt?"

"Yes. Could you imagine more calamaties on the head of one person?''

"What do you mean?"

"Do you know what it means to be Mrs. Bernhardt?''

"No.''

"It means to live with all the defects of the world. Did you ever stop to think that Mrs. Bernhardt is black? That she's old? Sick? Widowed? Alone? Jewish? And what's more, she's a woman! Seven reasons to be rejected, ignored, condemned, judged, punished. That's what it means to be Mrs. Bernhardt. But the worst part of it is that she doesn't rebel. She submits.''

I bit my lower lip. "I'm sorry . . . I—''

"Sorry? What are you talking about? Why sorry?''

"If I've caused you pain in one way or another.''

"That's not the point. You haven't understood a thing.''

"Oh, I see.'' Why was everyone taking me for an idiot these days?

"There's no point in being sorry. The point is to rebel.''

"Against what?''

"Against prejudices, against splendid morality. Against yourself, if you will. You, trembling at the thought that I'm going to pounce on you. Boy! Life is really revolting!'' Colin got up off his knees and sat down on the floor. "If there's something else that's bothering you, I'm here to listen.''

"Why did you allow yourself to be flayed by Hal?''

"Perhaps I just like it, as Bruce Conway would say.''

"Bruce is a specialist in stupid reactions.''

"Bruce is the only one around here who's really stripped of all meanness and all prejudice.'' Colin drew his knees up to his chin and wrapped his arms around them. "He treats people as equals. He makes fun of everyone indiscriminately.''

Holding out his left hand, he said, "Take my hand. Go on, take it."

"What for?"

"What lack of confidence! It's unbelievable!" He put his hand back on his knee. "You don't believe in a thing. What's there to it, your life?"

"How could that possibly matter to you?"

"It does matter. From time to time I find myself wondering, Where's Foster Tuncurry? I wonder if he's happy right at this moment. Then I say to myself: 'Has Bruce found a job?' Or else, 'Now how about that, there's Beatrice calling to Virgil in the stairway.' Yes, it does matter to me. Stairway C is at the heart of me. And maybe someday it will all stop and I'll be dead. Without Stairway C there's no Colin Shepherd. It's that simple."

"You haven't answered."

"Haven't answered what? Oh yes, Hal . . ." He chuckled softly, briefly. "I don't suppose there's anything to say."

"Easy to avoid the question!"

"If a guy who's twice as strong as you ties you up, stuffs a handkerchief in your mouth, dunks you in cold water, and cuts you into ribbons, I don't really see what you can do about it except get the floor wet."

"You weren't tied up, and you didn't have a handkerchief rammed down your throat."

"How should I know? I blacked out right away."

"You did manage to holler."

"Hey, why the third degree?"

"I'm trying to understand."

"Then go look up the police report. When Hal saw that I was out cold, he must have untied me. I woke up with a jolt and I screamed. At least that's what I think. I don't remember a thing."

"Still, you're obsessed by it."

"Who wouldn't be?"

"True enough," I admitted. "But what were you doing with that brute?"

"He wasn't always like that. But you would never understand. He couldn't bear to be homosexual. I pitied him."

"Pitied!"

"Yes, exactly. He was suffering. He took it out on me as best he could. At the time I had the extreme effrontery to be happy. How indecent!"

"And you're not that any longer? Happy?"

"What difference does it make?" he said.

For a moment I contemplated the drawings on the floor, hoping to find an answer there.

"In any case, this is sublime," I said. "Worse. It's beautiful."

"The scones are cold," he whispered with a disconcerting sense of the appropriate. "I'll make some more tomorrow. Will you come to have some at nine?"

Getting to my feet, I looked down at him.

"I suppose so."

"Help me up."

Colin reached out a hand, and I took it. Once on his feet, he withdrew it before I had the chance to let go.

"So, okay, see you tomorrow."

"See you tomorrow," I said.

For lunch that day I ventured out to an Italian restaurant. The waiter's endless chatter rubbed my nerves raw. What's more, the pasta wasn't *al dente,* and the meat sauce was right out of a can. I suspected the cook of being Chinese. Around two-fifteen I found myself with an empty head and empty hands but with my stomach heavily laden. So I decided to take a short digestive stroll wherever the streets might lead me. I soon realized that I was going in circles to the left. Therefore, I surmised, if lost in the desert, I would circle to the left, a stronger inclination in me than the right. And what if I were lost in the desert with a rightie? Would we manage to walk a straight line if we each guided by turns? Or would the strongest personality win out over the other?

It's odd how totally devoid of logic such inner conversations can be. I'd reached the point of asking myself what would happen if I should find myself with a right-footed dog when I was roughly shaken by the sleeve.

"You got something against artists?" rasped an aggressive voice.

I turned to face a tall girl holding a portfolio. "Why?" I asked. "Are you one?"

"So it would seem. Here, I'll show you."

Reluctantly I was dragged toward a street corner where other young people were congregated. An impromptu sidewalk art show was in progress.

Cheerlessly the young woman laid out the contents of her portfolio. I saw nothing but the usual horrors, the sun spots in acid-candy colors and geometric designs in black-and-white.

"That's it?"

"Yeah, that's it," she growled, immediately on the defensive.

I sighed.

"That, my child, isn't art. It's industrial production. You're all doing the same thing in the same way. Where's the creation in all of that?"

A pretty brunette with feathers dangling from her ears sidled up to us. "He's a troublemaker."

"A troublemaker? I should certainly hope so!" I cried. "If I could trouble you enough to make real artists of you, I'd at least have done one useful thing in my life."

"And what do you know about art?" raged the blue-eyed Indian maid as the others edged in closer.

"Good question. I'm very glad you asked it," I replied, moving resolutely away. "And my greetings to your parents, who must be really proud of you!"

"What's the matter with this guy? We're art students, not beggars."

"And that's not robbery?"

Behind me I heard someone laugh. A great, burly guy was coming at me with clenched fists.

"Come on, mister, don't be so nasty. They're still students. You can't blame them for earning pocket money to help with their schooling. Education doesn't come free, you know."

Spying a note pad and an art book under the man's arm, I beamed with pleasure. Here was an element that could, I hoped, play in my favor.

"You like Hieronymus Bosch, I see. Unless you're studying him at art school?"

"I'm not a student. I teach. As for Hieronymus Bosch, yes, I like him, and I do study him."

"Do you go along with the author's analysis?"

He looked at me with an expression of some surprise, which abruptly turned to mistrust.

"It's a good analysis, since you ask. Well documented but also very personal. Does that answer suit you?"

"Absolutely. Thank you. And I'll tell you why. Little Prairie Flower here asked me a moment ago what, if anything, I knew about art. What I know is right there." I touched the book with the tip of my finger. "A word to the wise—"

The professor grabbed me by the arm. "Reading your articles, I've often wondered what you were like, whether you were as caustic and cynical in real life. I've never been disappointed by your criticism. Your approach is unassailable in the literary and artistic domain. However, in conversation it is intolerable."

"I know, thank you. Someone is always giving me grief about it."

Without being rough about it I disengaged my arm. "Do you like Renoir?"

"Why not?" he said, raising one eyebrow.

"Yes. That's what I keep telling myself—why not? Never could think of anything else to say."

I gave a little goodbye wave and left with a smile on my face, willingly ignoring the last remark of the brunette with feathers: "Pretentious ass."

By six o'clock I felt in fine form and wicked enough to pop a few champagne corks. All set for the opening, I put on my dark gray suit and a black shirt, since the weather was as ready to storm as I was. I allowed myself one cigarette before leaving, aimlessly squaring up a few papers on my desk. And then the telephone rang.

"Hello?"

"Foster? Hi, it's James Coventry, *The Art Review.*"

"Sure, hi, James. How are things going?"

"Fine, thanks. Look here, would you like to do an article for us?"

"What do you have in mind?"

"Up to you. We're getting out a special issue devoted to one theme: water in painting, sculpture, and music. We're rather excited by it. What do you think?"

"It's pretty vast!"

"Well, give it some thought, then call me back and we'll talk terms. Okay?"

"Okay. Listen, how's the magazine doing?"

"You had to ask? Well, you could say we're hanging on. And what about you and Macland? You still muddling through with him?"

"Oh, you know Macland. . . . An article every three months, that's what he offers me. Hardly enough to make a living."

"Always wondered what you were living on, to tell the truth."

"You want to know my secret?"

"Yeah."

"Promise you won't laugh."

"I promise."

"Every month my father makes a deposit in Swiss francs in my bank account."

"You're kidding?"

"No, it's true. About a thousand bucks. With what I manage to earn from my articles, the lectures, and books, I'm not doing badly."

"A thousand? Look here, if your old man'd like to spread a little more around . . ."

"Actually he's never recovered from the fact that I didn't go for a career in the diplomatic service the way he did; but he swells with pride whenever he sees Tuncurry on the spine of a book. He just wants to assure himself that I'm not living in misery. The family honor is at stake."

"If only I could weasel a paltry five dollars out of my parents! They practically make me pay for the meal when I go to see them."

"I don't even have to see mine. They live in Switzerland."

"Some luck! Look here, you wouldn't like to make a generous contribution to *The Art Review?*"

"I'm already doing articles without pay."

"That's an exaggeration. We paid the last time."

"Yes. Merely six months later. A record."

"We do what we can. Look here, were you invited to the Contemporary Arts Day on the sixteenth?"

"No. What is it?"

"Oh, some sort of gathering with a few panels. It's organized by some people at Columbia."

"It's all news to me."

"Like an invitation? We've got a bundle of them here."

"As spectator or participant?"

"Spectator. But there's sure to be some old bozo who'll ask you to make a few brief remarks."

"Oh, well, send it along."

"Will do. Now, look here, enough of this gabfest. I've got work to do."

"No kidding!"

As I hung up I congratulated myself on my restraint. I had resisted the desire to toss a "look here" or two back at James.

It was getting late. Hurrying downstairs, I found Mrs. Bernhardt in front of her mailbox. Since her back was turned, I slipped by without a greeting. But once out the door, I felt pangs of remorse and turned back.

"Good evening, Mrs. Bernhardt."

She gave a start and looked at me anxiously.

"Ah, Mr. Tuncurry."

"Is something the matter?"

"Uh . . . my key is stuck."

"Here, let me try."

I got the key out without much trouble.

"Thank you, Mr. Tuncurry. That was so kind of you."

"It's really nothing at all. Hope you have a nice evening."

"Thank you. . ."

This time I took off again at top speed. Luckily I caught a cab just going by. When I reached the Schmidt Gallery, I thought I wouldn't be able to get in. A real horror show. I shuddered and pushed aside a small fat figure in front of me to get by.

He turned around, indignant. "Your invitation?" he shouted, as though demanding my passport.

I held out my card. He calmed down.

"There are so many gate crashers."

"You should be pleased."

"Oh, but they're only coming for the buffet. And at that, if you want something to eat, you'd better hurry up. My God, the heat's awful."

"There's going to be a thunderstorm. You want me to bring you a drink?"

"Thanks, that's awfully nice of you. If you could find a bit of Perrier, I'd really like that, Mr., Mr. . . .?"

"Foster Tuncurry."

"Really?"

"That's what it says on the invitation."

"Oh, I didn't read it. Very pleased to meet you. I'm Julius Schmidt. Just the nephew. Of Sigmund Schmidt."

"Why just the nephew?" I asked with a laugh, after stepping

forward, then backward, jostled by a sudden movement of the crowd.

"Oh, I'm not at all important here. As you see, I'm the one they put at the door."

"And the show, what do you think of it?"

"Oh, me and painting . . . My real passion is for scale models."

"Well, now, that's amusing."

"You think so?" His shy, fleeting smile made him sympathetic.

"But I'm forgetting, I promised you a Perrier. I'll be back as soon as I can."

"No hurry."

Taking a deep breath, I dove into the moving mass of bodies. Julius Schmidt waved in what looked strangely like a farewell. I wondered if, in fact, I would ever reemerge from the ocean of inane laughter, greasy fingers, and lapels drenched in whiskey.

Attempting to catch a glimpse of the paintings between the heads, I vaguely made out a few round, blue forms. After cubism you have circularism . . . not my lucky day. Always horrified by polka-dot material, here I was confronted with nothing but polka-dot canvases. I could feel the resurgence of my familiar demonic spirit. My kindness used up on Julius, make way for my instinctive nastiness! Cost what it might, I'd snatch a Perrier from them—even at the price of trampling their toes and digging my elbows into tender flesh. What's more, I had vowed to myself that I would pin down the gallery's publicity agent. Swept along with the current of intrepid buffet-goers, I ultimately spirited off two brimming glasses from under the nose of a character in white who threw me a dirty look. In the distance, between a bare shoulder and a hat, I spotted Sigmund Schmidt, pudgy and glistening with sweat—or was it pretension? He was conversing with an elegantly attired young woman and Mrs. Ariboska, the terror of cocktail parties. I quickly looked away in the fear that she might notice me. Almost by chance I got back to the door and Julius. I held out his glass with the modest pride befitting a conqueror of the Himalayas.

"Oh, thanks. My, but that was quick!"

"You think so?"

"You caught a glimpse of the paintings?"

"Alas, yes!"

"You don't like them?"

"No."

"So you're going to give an unfavorable review?"

This idea seemed to give Julius a certain pleasure.

"I'd rather not write at all. They're not even worth a bad review. What if we talked instead about scale models?"

"Oh, it's a mistake to get me going on that one! You'll never turn me off."

"I can always turn off anyone I please."

"Well, in that case . . . my favorites are Spitfires. Believe it or not, I've built more than two hundred and sixty of them, going from less than three inches to eleven-and-a-half feet."

"Eleven-and-a-half feet! This hobby of yours takes up a good bit of space."

"Yes, I guess it does. And then, you see . . ."

I had abruptly stopped listening to Julius. By some unexpected good fortune, Sigmund Schmidt and his pretty companion were free of Mrs. Ariboska. I interrupted Julius, who was onto wing struts.

"Tell me, who is that young woman with your uncle?"

"That . . . uh, wait a minute . . . yes, it's Miss Fairchild, our publicist."

"Perfect. Excuse me, my friend, I must exchange a few words with them."

I slipped between two backs, dodged a *foie gras* on toast, and planted my feet firmly in front of Sigmund Schmidt. He gave me a look of obvious pleasure.

"Why, Mr. Tuncurry! I did not dare hope for the pleasure of your company!"

"As a matter of fact, you all but didn't have it. I got the invitation only yesterday. Those publicity people! It's unbelievable. They have nothing else to think about, and yet they always do everything wrong! You have press releases available, I trust?"

"Uh, no."

Seeing Sigmund Schmidt disconcerted, I pressed on. "Not a solitary press release! You may say that for gallery shows they aren't necessary. But when I do an article, I want the full, correct information, as you well know." Then, with my most charming smile, I gallantly held out my hand to the young lady at my side. "But I do rattle on . . . and you haven't introduced me!"

Sigmund glanced at me anxiously as he blurted, "Ms. Fairchild."

Her chin shot up, and she spoke distinctly, no doubt thinking to make me squirm. "Florence Fairchild, director of publicity."

Refusing to take notice, I turned like a perfect cad to speak to Sigmund, as though she weren't there.

"I met your nephew. Such a pleasant time."

"My nephew? Oh, yes, Julius."

Sigmund began to quaver on the pair of pins that held up his bowling ball of a body. This time he looked frankly distraught. Florence Fairchild decided to take up the offensive.

"But you haven't said what you think of the works on display."

"What works?" I replied without blinking.

"What do you mean, what works? Why these, of course."

Ms. Fairchild tried to make a sweeping gesture, but her arm met too many obstacles. I stared at her for a moment or two, not hesitating to take in her shoes; her black-and-white dress; the low neckline of her dress, which showed off her breasts to good advantage; her curly auburn hair; and her strawberry-hued lips. Total stupefaction was written across her face.

"Do you take me for an idiot?" I said with a Bruce Conway smile. "Are you asking me about the crap that's smeared on these walls?"

Florence Fairchild suddenly went crimson. "You are the most disagreeable individual I've ever met!"

"And hypocritical! Terribly hypocritical," I added. "But you should know, *dear* Ms. Fairchild, that a press rep is one who, by definition, never loses her cool. You are distinctly unsuited to the job. And you, *dear* Mr. Schmidt, do be kind enough to tell your paint-dabblers to take up music. When they observe the audience plugging their ears, they will understand the degree to which they are unsuited to painting."

I bowed from the waist. On the way out I tapped Julius on the shoulder and we exchanged farewells. It had begun to drizzle. I walked home. As I passed the liquor store I bought four bottles of wine in anticipation of our monthly dinner at Bruce's. I always take care of the wine. Colin brings the first course, Beatrice the dessert, and Bruce and Virgil collaborate on the main dish.

I passed no one on my way up the steps of Stairway C.

3. Dinner at Bruce's

That morning I woke up with The Idea. I leaped to the phone and called James Coventry, who enthusiastically accepted my article in advance. I set to work immediately, but at nine-fifteen I suddenly remembered promising to have breakfast with Colin. I threw on some clothes and reached the fourth floor at the very moment Colin opened his door.

He laughed. "I was just coming down to look for you!"

"Sorry, but I'm seething with excitement."

"Oh, really? Why?"

"I have an article to do. I'd barely started when I remembered that I was coming up here. So . . . ."

"So?"

"So nothing. Here I am. Late, but here."

"Well, come and sit down instead of carrying on about it."

"Just as you say, sir. Something smells great!"

"Black coffee and toasted scones."

"Ah, the poetry of it."

Colin started to laugh again, somewhat nervously. I got the impression that he was preoccupied. His playfulness seemed false. He lit up a cigarette and began to smoke while pouring the coffee. He got up for a moment to get the scones and butter. I watched him with surprise.

"You're smoking now?"

"What?" He started violently, as though he had been caught with his hand in the till.

"You're smoking?"

"Yes. I stopped a long time ago and then . . . well, I suddenly had a hankering for it."

"Oh, I see. You know, Colin, things don't seem to be going so well for you this morning. Is something wrong?"

"Oh, no, no. It's not that. . . . It's . . ."

"It's?"

"Nothing. A touch of the blues, perhaps. By tonight I'll be better."

"Speaking of tonight, have you given some thought to the first course?"

"First course? Ah, yes. For the dinner. Well, uh, no."

"Your head's really in the clouds today."

He smiled sadly. I anxiously downed my scone in one mouthful. Perhaps I'd been too rough on him the day before, had hurt him. I racked my brains for something to say.

"All you have to do is buy something or other at the Greek's. He's got everything."

"What?"

"The Greek. The entrée for the meal at Bruce's. Hey, there! Are you awake?"

"Ah, the Greek. You bet. Sure, I'll go there, right."

He was absently sipping his coffee.

"You're sure you feel okay, Shep?"

"Yeah, sure, I'm okay. I just need to get up a little head of steam."

But he only slowed down, as if running in slow motion. Then he bounded to his feet.

"Well, that's it for now," he declared. "I've really got to get moving!"

He snatched up his jacket and slipped into both sleeves at once. Popping a scone into my mouth, he firmly shoved me out the door. Then he dashed downstairs, throwing back a "See you tonight." I was speechless.

Title: Water in the *Ocean Vessels* Series, *The Storm at Sea, Landscape with the Fall of Icarus,* Brueghel the Elder. Illustrations: *Naval Combat in the Straits of Messina, Armed Three-Masted Ship, The Storm at Sea, The Fall of Icarus* (prints).
Quotation: "The sun shone
As it had to on the white legs disappearing into the green
Water."—*Musée des Beaux Arts,* W. H. Auden.
"These lines from W. H. Auden were inspired by *Ic-*

arus, and what is more marvelous than a pictorial work
that 'intrigues the art historians and enthuses the poets,'
as Philip Robert-Jones put it?''

I had to stop typing in order to get up, jump around and shout
a bit, to let off steam so I wouldn't explode. My head was teem-
ing with so many ideas that it would have taken a book to use
them all up, and I had spent the day trying to compress them
into five pages. I was mentally exhausted.

At seven o'clock I left my worktable to go up to Bruce's
apartment. From the doorstep I caught a few notes of music that
made me smile. I rang. Beatrice opened the door.
"The Fan Club of the *Adagio Assai,* I presume?"
"Password?" she said gravely as the music swelled.
"Ravel, *Concerto in G,* 1930."
"Good, that'll do for this time."
I found Virgil and Bruce in deep debate. Bruce broke off in
mid-sentence and came over.
"What did you bring for wine?" he asked.
"The usual."
"How boring."
"Tough. You can always drink water, you know."
"Water? Never heard of such a thing."
He sat down and picked up where he had left off. "As far as
that goes, the whole thing's pure bunk."
"Wha?" said Virgil.
"I say it's bunk, all that stuff about astrology, esoterica,
Cabala . . . gibberish."
"You don't know a thing about it, and besides, you're get-
ting it all mixed up," said Virgil with an exaggerated frown of
despair.
I sat down near the turntable and gave myself up to the music, sensing the power of the *Adagio Assai* on a physical level. I
could feel gooseflesh rising with the orchestra, and a paralysis
that took its lead from the piano. I stayed there, staring off into
space, breathing to the tempo of the piece. The sound of the
oboe wove through my head; I felt a sort of stabbing pain at
the back of the skull as the piano reclaimed the foreground.
The sweetness of the strings soothed my ragged senses. I
stopped the record before the third movement, whose brutality

would have been too much to bear. In its place I flipped the record to *Concerto for the Left Hand,* which was frenzied enough to bring me out of my torpor.

"Terrible, eh?" whispered Beatrice in a voice suddenly gone hoarse.

"This one isn't bad," I replied.

"Yeah, but the *other one* . . ."

"I know."

We knew indeed.

"It's even more beautiful than Debussy."

"Perfection is hard to take," I said with a sigh.

"How true!"

"Whoa there! Let's not have any of that crap, okay?"

At Bruce's remark we both turned to look at him.

"Kindly tell this dimwit that he's taken leave of his senses," he said to me.

The torment of the concerto had left me temporarily speechless.

"I've no idea what you're talking about."

"Bah, doesn't matter, anyway."

And they went back to their conversation. I stayed beside Beatrice, listening till the end of the record. In this area we had perfect understanding, she and I. Bruce was watching us furtively.

"Is this what they feed to cows so they'll give more milk?" he asked me.

Beatrice groaned.

"You've got him mixed up with Beethoven," I said. "And Wagner makes beans grow."

Bruce frowned and assumed a gravity that gave promise of worse yet to come.

"Yes, but what does the Jewish Cabala have to say about it? First of all, are beans sensitive to the cycles of the moon, and do they confront their destiny in an esoteric fashion? Does the tin can remain neutral if it is domiciled within the Capricorn? And finally, your Wagner wasn't even Jewish! It smacks of a contradiction, my dear Professor Schmuck!"

"Oh, shut the fuck up!" shouted Virgil, though he couldn't help laughing. "Good God, but he's idiotic!"

The door bell rang. As usual Colin was the last to arrive.

"Good, maybe we can sit down to eat now that the first

course has arrived,'' Bruce declared, pushing me toward a corner of the sofa. "You sit there."

"Is that an order?" I asked.

"Absolutely. Sit!"

I found myself beside Colin and his mushrooms *à la Grecque,* a sublime representation of false ethnic cuisine.

"Some music, maestro," I requested.

"Give us *The Rite of Spring,*" Colin entreated.

"Oh, no . . . not that again," I protested. "I already get to hear it every morning. Enough's enough! What about something at least remotely contemporary?"

Bruce chose a record off the shelf and lowered the volume. Soon Tangerine Dream was wafting around us, discreet and well mannered.

"What were you talking about before I got here?" Colin inquired.

"About beans," Bruce replied.

"Splendid subject. But what else?"

"About cows and Beethoven."

"Not bad, either."

"Beethoven is just fine. I don't see what's so funny about Beethoven!" Virgil protested.

"That's true," I said. "There's nothing funny about Beethoven, nothing at all."

"Well, I happen to like Beethoven," he answered.

"Sure, cows do too."

"Oh, spare us your cows!"

Virgil scooped some mushrooms onto his plate.

"Who said that 'laughter is the attribute of man'?" Bruce inquired.

"Bergson," I replied.

"Well, that's pure rot."

"Really, why?"

"Just look at Virgil's face and draw your own conclusion."

The face in question was turning glummer by the second. Bruce was about to open his mouth again when I gave him a kick to shut him up. His trouble is that he never knows when to stop, and since Virgil is the sensitive type . . .

Colin was first to break the silence. "What about your article? Is it going well?"

"Even a bit too well! I'm going at a hundred ideas a minute.'' I smiled and went on. ''The problem is in squeezing it all into five pages. But do be kind, all of you; don't get me started on that. I've had enough of it for today.''

''Do I understand correctly that this spells the end of culture in our conversation for this evening?'' asked Bruce. ''So what'll we go to next? Politics? Movies? The latest eat-fest? Women? Perhaps wine?''

''Instead let's go to the next course,'' suggested Beatrice.

Bruce simply changed the subject. ''This afternoon I ran into a little brunette selling her canvases on Waverly Place. A really cute chick.''

Beatrice pursed her lips and glowered at Bruce Conway, who went right on with even greater enthusiasm.

''And you know what? She had feathers tucked behind her ears! Some foxy babe!''

''Amazing,'' I said. ''I know her too. She has gorgeous blue eyes.''

''That's right!''

''Yes, and if I remember correctly, she called me a trouble-maker and a pretentious ass. You could say we don't share the same point of view. . . .''

''That's a pretty good summing up of your personality,'' remarked Virgil.

''I never denied it. . . .''

''You have to admit that her work wasn't all that great. But the feathers . . . so sexy!''

''So you said,'' retorted Beatrice with barely concealed contempt.

''And I'll repeat it! So-o sexy!''

Bruce raised his eyes to the ceiling, then let out a long whistle.

''The next chick I take out will have to wear feathers to bed. And what's more, they'll have to tickle!''

Colin burst out laughing. ''What lunacy!''

''Oh, yeah? We all have our fantasies, no?''

''Splendid!'' I said. ''Do tell us your fantasies, Bruce.''

''To be quite frank my greatest fantasy had to do with Suzy. You know, Suzy . . . that dubious lady Foster would treat himself to from time to time. I always wondered what it would be like to have a woman who looked so stupid. It fascinated me that Tuncurry could come up with something like that. I dreamed about it, just from trying to imagine what it would be like in bed. I never could be sure. So, how was it, Foster?''

"Colossally boring," I answered.

"This is unbelievable! He dares to admit it! So, what was there in it for you?"

"It's absolutely indispensable to be bored from time to time. It enhances the active moments by contrast. At any rate, screwing is like eating—it's necessary, but it's rarely very good.''

"What a cynic you can be! It's like a vice with you. Simply mind-boggling!''

Bruce looked at me quizzically. "Sometimes I wonder if you get any joy out of life. I often have the feeling that everything bores you.''

"Actually you're right. Everything does bore me.''

"Did you ever consider suicide?''

"Yes, but that would be just as boring. And besides, I'm a coward.''

Beatrice picked up her knife and rapped on her plate. "I'm hungry!''

"Yes, yes, we're on our way," grumbled Bruce as he reluctantly got to his feet.

I had the very distinct impression that we were not through with that subject, he and I, but that it would be continued another day. I knew perfectly well that I was an enigma to Bruce Conway. And in a certain measure it was reciprocal.

"What are you reading now?" I asked Virgil.

"Herzog."

"Oh, yeah. Saul Bellow. *Herzog* is the one where the guy keeps writing letters that he never sends?''

"Yes, that's the one. It's not bad.''

"That's all?''

"Well, you know me. Aside from *Wuthering Heights* . . .''

"That's true, you are the great romantic.''

"And here it is!" Bruce exclaimed. "For madame, chicken marinara.'' He put the platter down right in front of Beatrice.

But she wrinkled her nose and replied, "That's all you could find? Zero for originality!''

"Okay, don't make us sweat for it. If you're not satisfied, there's always the restaurant, little lady!''

"So there is, so there is. . . .''

Colin was helping himself without ceremony. "Well, frankly, I'm starved."

Undertaking to serve everyone, he put a double portion on Beatrice's plate.

"My diet!"

"What about it? You're skinny as a rail."

"I rather like her that way," said Virgil with a smile.

"Gotta admit you're not exactly fat, either."

"In this assembly no one is any better than the other," Bruce remarked. "Look at me. . . ."

"No, thanks," said Beatrice. "We'd lose our appetites."

But Bruce Conway had risen to his feet and was barging ahead. "C'mon, look at me. I'm thin, but it's all muscle. Not like that shrimp, Virgil Sparks."

"And what about me?" I asked as Bruce was pulling off his shirt. "Am I skinny?"

"You? You're soft. Now get a look at this." Bare-chested, Bruce began to strike classic physical-culture poses. Beatrice smothered a laugh behind her napkin.

"There's no denying," she managed to say, "*that* has a very intelligent look about it!"

But nothing was going to cut short Bruce's exhibition.

"Now when it comes to thighs and calves . . ."

He unbuckled his belt but froze as he caught Colin's expression. Turning that way, I, too, was struck by his pale face and the look in his eye. Bruce was quick to sit down, saying that his meat was getting cold. For a moment we ate in silence, then Bruce and I took up our conversation again.

"I went by your apartment yesterday," he said, "but you weren't there."

"No, I went to an art show. Deplorable, but I had a good time. You wanted to see me?"

"Yes. I mean, no."

"Yes or no?"

"Maybe."

"So which was it?"

"I don't remember. I must have had some reason, but now I've forgotten."

"What absolutely gripping conversation!" bantered Virgil as he gulped down an enormous chunk of chicken.

"Got something better to offer?" I asked.

Virgil, his mouth full, couldn't answer.

"See, you don't have a thing to say," I added with satisfaction.

Virgil half choked, trying to swallow more quickly. As he began to cough Bruce laughed.

"If you could just see your face!"

Virgil shook a fist at him but only coughed harder.

"Go stand on your hands. That usually works," I advised him half-facetiously.

Virgil downed a tall glass of water and poured the last droplets on Bruce's sleeve. He heaved a sigh of relief.

"Whew, that's better."

Placidly Bruce flicked the water off with his hand. "Did he do it on purpose?" he asked, knitting his brows.

"For the rest of your life you'll be wondering," Virgil replied.

"I'm certainly going to lose sleep over it."

"I do hope so!"

"Ah, yes, now I know!" Bruce suddenly shouted.

"Beg your pardon?"

"I remember why I came by your place yesterday."

"Oh, good. Why?"

"I wanted to borrow some money."

"Lucky I wasn't there!"

"Makes no difference. You can give me some today."

"Oh, really?"

"Optimism is lovely to behold," said Beatrice.

"Terribly sorry, my friend, but I cannot lend you any money at the moment."

"But I have to pay the rent."

"Me, too, you know."

"Sparks? Can you?"

"Out of the question. I'm not too sure how I'm going to swing it myself."

Bruce didn't dare ask Beatrice, but Colin volunteered on his own.

"Hey, thanks!" Bruce said fervently.

"You don't realize what you're getting into," I cautioned. "You should know that Bruce never borrows money, he takes it."

"And then?" retorted the interested party.

"And then? You owe me more than two hundred."

"Oh, my God, I'd forgotten."

"Well . . ."

"I can pay you back if you need it," Colin spoke up.

"What?"

"Yes, it wouldn't put me out. And that way Bruce would be in debt to only one person. It would simplify the accounting."

I couldn't hide my surprise. "What unexpected generosity!"

"Why? After all, if anyone had asked me earlier, I'd gladly have loaned some money. It just never came up. I'm fairly well off."

"That's good to know!" Bruce remarked, giving me a quizzical look to which I couldn't reply.

I began to suspect Colin of being in love with Bruce Conway. It bothered and worried me without my knowing quite why. But if Bruce became Colin's debtor and was unable to repay him, Colin might look for a moral hold over him. However, this was no more than supposition, and there was nothing to prove that Colin was harboring any such idea.

"At any rate, I don't need your two hundred," I concluded.

"But I assure you it wouldn't bother me."

"It would me," I answered firmly. My severe tone prompted an uncomfortable hush for a few moments.

"You seen any good movies recently, Virgil?" Bruce finally inquired.

"Movies these days make me want to puke!"

"Nice dinner talk!" noted Beatrice. "May I take consolation in the dessert I've been preparing with tender loving care all afternoon?"

"What is it?" I asked.

"A cheesecake."

"Strawberry?"

"I wouldn't stoop so low!"

"Well, thank heavens."

"If you want it, why not go and get it?" proposed Bruce with a modicum of good humor.

Muttering to herself, Beatrice got to her feet.

"While you're up," Bruce added, "do change the record. . . ."

"Anything else?"

"That'll do for now."

44

Then, turning back to Virgil, Bruce said, "Let's get back to fantasies. I told you mine; now for the rest of you. Your turn, Foster!"

"Me? Well . . . how about my dream of meeting Ronald Reagan face-to-face."

"Eh?"

"Yeah . . . there he is, coming toward me with his four-square smile, hand out. And he says to me, 'Here he is, our dear Mr. Tuncurry, the very flower of our beloved country. . . .' "

"And then?"

"Then? Nothing."

"What d'you mean, nothing?"

"Nothing. I'd turn my back without shaking his hand. That's all."

"Fascinating. Do I detect a certain contempt for authority and the establishment?"

"Not in the least. Simply contempt for Reagan."

"Me, I love Reagan," whispered Bruce Conway. "He's handsome, bright-eyed, erect of bearing. And then he's gotta be real intelligent or he wouldn't be president."

"Intelligent? You said it! Regular genius!" I replied. "The proof is, he's the only one who understands Reaganomics, right?"

"Yup . . . okay, next fantasy. Virgil?"

"No idea."

"Really? Give it a try!"

"I'd settle for running Boorman through with one of his plastic swords, still dripping from *Excalibur.* "

"We're not going to start talking about *Excalibur,* are we?" Beatrice snapped.

"Ask me for a fantasy and I'll give you one, Marm!"

"Splendid," she said, "and if you'd like to know mine, it would be to shove Virgil Sparks into the bear cage at the Central Park Zoo."

"Have pity on the poor animals!" I exclaimed. "Now for you, Colin."

"I dream that Bruce Conway finds a job in a bank and has to wear a suit and tie and be nice to the customers. It would be wildly funny."

"Strange, I see him rather as a liveried chauffeur, holding

his cap by the visor as he opens the door. 'If your Lordship would kindly—' "

"That's it, you two!" Bruce protested. "I mean, really! Just get a load of these idiots having a high old time at my expense!"

True enough, Colin and I were doubled over with laughter, realizing that we had come up with similar ideas at the expense of Bruce Conway. It proved contagious, and soon the others were laughing along with us, even Bruce himself.

"That's ridiculous!" he said with a sigh, putting an end to it.

"I suppose that's one of the earmarks of a fantasy," I replied.

"Being ridiculous?"

"Yes."

"Really! A chauffeur . . . Just you wait, I'll get even!"

Beatrice had put on the *Brandenburg Concertos* as background music. I grimaced.

"Who's conducting?" I asked.

"What?"

"The Bach."

"Wait a sec, uh . . ." Bruce got up to look on the jacket. "Leppard."

"Thought so," I couldn't help saying. "It's no good."

"You're so difficult!"

"Damn right, I'm difficult. But I can only take this kind of thing when it's done right. In other words, Harnoncourt or nothing."

"Yeah, and for Monteverdi, Clemencic or nothing," Beatrice added.

"Correct."

"What snobs, those two," Virgil noted. "The moment it has to do with music, we're all demented and they're always right."

"And why not?" Beatrice replied. "Music is my domain. I gladly leave you the movies."

"Coffee, anyone?" Bruce inquired with a yawn.

"You, it would seem," I said.

He gave me his lopsided grin and a wink. "It's not that I'm tired, it's just that you're beginning to bore the bejeezus out of me."

"Always so agreeable!"

"Me, I'd like some coffee," said Colin, all but mealy-mouthed.

"Okay, two coffees. Bea?"

"No, thanks."

"Virgil? There's three . . . and Foster as always. That makes four. I'm on my way."

As Bruce went off to the kitchen he added, "Beatrice, since you're not having coffee, how about doing the dishes."

"Say it again? I didn't get that!"

"Forget it," I put in quickly, hoping to avoid a scene. "Colin and I will do it. Come on, let's go."

Colin followed me obediently, and we began to wash up while waiting for the coffee. When Bruce left for a moment to get the cups out of his sideboard, I took the opportunity to exchange a few words with Colin, who was drying the dishes with a practiced hand.

"You seem better than this morning," I began. "Though you're still not exactly garrulous."

"Um . . . yes."

"You're sure nothing's wrong?"

"Yes . . . I . . ." He looked at me with a strange expression that seemed to betray some fear or anxiety.

"What's the matter, Colin?"

Alas, at the very moment his lips began to move, Bruce came back to get the sugar and check the percolator.

4. *Intermezzo*

That morning I'd have tossed the whole thing out the window if I could. Above me the Rachmaninoff *Opus 4* was going at a hundred decibels; next door Virgil and Beatrice were flailing each other at about five hundred decibels; and downstairs a brat was hollering at her mother loud enough to be heard above the whole hullabaloo. I was about to go deaf. I went onto the landing and let off a bellow so as not to feel excluded.

A voice wafted down from the fifth floor. "Things not going too well, eh?" Bruce, in shorts, was contributing to the din.

When an "Excuse me, please" rose from below, I was surprised to see a young woman on the second floor with a little girl and an armful of baggage in tow.

I made an effort to be nice. "Yes?"

"I'm terribly sorry my daughter made such a racket. Normally she's not a crier, I assure you. You won't be disturbed. . . . It's just the moving and all that. It upsets her."

The argument in Virgil's apartment started up again even louder than before, and our new tenant seemed astonished at the vehemence of the words. I reassured her as best I could.

"Don't worry. It's always like this. It wasn't your daughter I was mad at, anyway. But between the musical maniac on the fourth and the pair of imbeciles next door—"

I was rudely jostled by Bruce as he bounded downstairs.

"Really, you boor! The lady could use a hand."

I caught up with him as he reached the last step.

"Hi! I'm Bruce Conway. The abominable one is Foster Tuncurry, and the two you hear bellowing are Virgil Sparks and Beatrice Holt. She's your neighbor. As for Rachmaninoff, his real name is Colin Shepherd. We're a sort of commune, you might say. Matter of fact, you wouldn't have a spare tenner, Foster?''

''No.''

''See what I mean? We're mutually supportive.''

His lopsided grin, his darting glance, his shorts and running shoes . . . yes, Bruce was really irresistible.

''I'm Sharon Dowd, and this is my daughter Anita.''

With an alacrity that I deemed suspect, Bruce offered his services—and mine. So I was drafted for the transport of cartons. Sharon Dowd must have been around thirty or thirty-five, with very long chestnut hair and pretty, black eyes. She seemed shy and awkward, or at any rate, totally dumbfounded by the voluble exuberance of Bruce Conway, who was overdoing everything. Little Anita was attentively observing my every gesture with such brazen intensity that I began to avoid her eye for fear of blushing. Finally, after a quick glance at the frenetic one who was taking up her mother's full attention, she flung back a lock of blond hair with a remarkably flirtatious gesture and, from the full height of her five years, tossed one word at me.

''Daddy.''

Recoiling in surprise, I bumped into a suitcase and fell flat on the ground. Bruce guffawed while Sharon asked me whether I had hurt myself. Swearing as I got to my feet, I felt desperation gaining on me, for Anita was still studying me gravely and, worse still, in a calculating manner. With totally feminine aplomb she struck again.

''Want to be my daddy?''

''Anita!''

Sharon Dowd turned crimson with shame. This time Bruce tactfully stifled his impulse to burst out laughing. But the horrid child persevered.

''But he's the one *I* want!''

''Really, Anita, you're talking nonsense!''

''But I want him.''

''We're just wondering what you see in him,'' declared Bruce.

She hesitated momentarily, appearing to reflect, then delivered her prime argument.

''It's not fair that Mommy always gets to choose!''

I thought the mother might faint. She stammered, tried to apologize for her daughter, angrily rolled her eyes at her, and, totally undone, turned back to Bruce. Who said nothing. So I was obliged to take up the defense. Crouching in front of the child, I met her moist eyes.

"Anita, I have no desire to be your daddy."

"Why?"

"Because you can't be the daddy of someone you don't know."

"Then what about the other daddies?"

I had no idea what to say.

"Mommy chooses the other ones. This is the one I want."

She dug a finger into my shoulder in total defiance of her mother.

"Why me? Why not that other one?"

"No. You."

I gave up. Miserable, Sharon was wilting in the arms of Bruce Conway, who seemed rather pleased with the turn of events.

"Oh, God, I'm sorry, I'm so sorry. . . . What must you think of me?"

"Given that all of us are pretty much damaged goods in this place, you shouldn't get too overwrought about it. Really."

Anita was visibly racking her brain for ways to convince us of her rights over my person. Eventually she declared, most poetically, "He has eyes like oysters, and I like oysters."

From this I deduced that her favorite color was gray.

Through their wide-open door I could see the Holt-Sparks ménage, who stopped their coming and going long enough to emerge and introduce themselves.

"So now, are you both done with the verbal abuse for the time being?" I asked, still attended by Anita.

Blushing, Virgil finally stammered, "Oh . . . a slight altercation perhaps."

"Slight?" Beatrice was quick to interpose. "Foster, you're my witness—"

"No, no! I'm not going to get involved."

"Just listen, at least! All I said was that it was idiotic for each of us to keep up an apartment. It's costing us plenty, and that's just plain stupid these days. . . . This cretin won't hear of it. You know why?"

"No."

"Me, neither."

"It's because he uses it for entertaining his numerous mistresses," quipped Bruce.

"That must be it," Beatrice responded.

"Well, I've got to go," concluded Virgil, taking off with dispatch.

Disconsolate, Beatrice shrugged. "Me, too. Goodbye, Sharon. Goodbye, Anita. So long, you two bears."

She also disappeared, quite evidently dismayed. Sharon was no longer weeping and, after thanking us, tried to put us out the door. But Bruce had decided to unpack the cartons, and nothing would dissuade him. I stayed out of sympathy for Sharon, whom I judged to be in some danger of seduction. Anita sat herself down on the floor and began to play with a doll. From time to time I caught her eye, invincible and full of reproach. I tried to disregard her mute presence but detected her scent wafting all around me. It may seem strange, but for me Anita had a perfume, something like amber—tenacious, indestructible, and obsessive. Eventually exasperated by the whole thing, I abandoned the weakling of a mother to the wily Bruce Conway, to his evident relief. What came of it between them, I have no idea.

Colin had replaced Rachmaninoff with Stravinsky. Taking this as an appeal, I went directly to his apartment. He seemed very pleased to see me. I told him about my first contact with the new tenants on the second, leaning heavily on the fact that Bruce was doing nothing to disguise his interest in the lovely Sharon. Colin didn't seem much impressed. On the other hand, the picture I drew of Anita prompted an arresting comment. He saw the child as a sort of opposite to the mother. She was strong, authoritarian, not to say pitiless. Even cruel, I added to myself. In short, a kind of black duplicate of a white original. While Colin poured me a cup of coffee I asked how he felt this morning.

"I'm fine. Why?"

"Because yesterday . . ."

"Oh, well, yesterday was yesterday."

I concluded that I would get nothing out of him.

"You working today?"

"No . . . I'm going to paint."

"Aha! Good."

He laughed. "Your wicked eye lights up! I'm not sure I like that."

It was my turn to laugh, then I stood up and went to the window.

"It doesn't look too bad out. I think I'll go take a walk. You want to come along?"

For a moment he raised his eyes from the floor and studied my face. Slowly his lips spread in a smile. I saw in it the unfolding of unexpected pleasure, a sort of triumph, almost a possessiveness.

But he declined my offer. Annoyed, I hastened my departure. Colin didn't budge but vaguely waved as he took a sip of coffee. I slammed the door louder than necessary.

On leaving Colin's place I went back to my apartment to change. When I'm in a bad humor, I like to be well dressed. Seduce and please, so as to wreak all the more havoc. I put on my gorgeous tan suede suit and a brown hem-stitched shirt, which I left open at the neck to show off the ID chain I occasionally wear. Pausing to admire my reflection in the mirror, I cleverly mussed my hair so that a dark curl fell across my right eye.

I left Stairway C with a feeling of immense satisfaction, abetted by the fact that people gazed with envy as I passed. Digging my hands deep into the pockets of my trousers, I slowed my pace to a saunter.

At a busy corner of Washington Square Park, I found a small cluster of young people. I recognized my art students. The pretty squaw was still wearing her feathers. I stopped in front of a watercolor precariously propped on the pavement. They turned toward me as one; our previous encounter had quite obviously not been forgotten.

"Say, there's Dean Martin," said the Indian.

I instantly tossed my hair back into place.

"How's it going?" I responded, as though we were all old friends. Slowly and deliberately crouching down in front of the painting, I took hold and tilted it to eliminate a reflection. It was a delicately painted landscape, blue-green and right angles.

"I suppose you don't like it?" the little lovely went on.

"It's not awfully new," I suggested. "Once there was this guy called Cézanne . . ."

"You know about him? I'd have thought your knowledge ended with the eighteenth century."

"Why is that?" I asked with a shrug.

"Because you don't seem to like contemporary art."

"You're entirely mistaken. If that were the case, I wouldn't wear myself out criticizing it."

I read the signature on the work, simply a first name.

"Who is this Vanessa?" I inquired, hoping it would be she.

"I'm Vanessa. Vanessa Poretski."

"Poretski?"

"You've got something against Poles?"

"Are you related to the communist revolutionary?"

"Eh?"

"The one who was rubbed out by the NKVD in thirty-seven?"

"So my father claims. My mother is American. How come you know about that?"

"Oh, I know a great many more things than you're willing to grant me, my child."

I saw her frown reprovingly. "I'm not your child."

After a moment's hesitation she timidly asked my opinion of her watercolor.

"It would be gorgeous hanging on the wall between the provincial sideboard and the grandfather clock. . . . Don't take that as a final judgment," I was quick to add. "It's sweet, it's decorative, it's well done."

"But?"

"But I don't like things that are content to be pretty or agreeable. I expect something more from you. Perhaps I'm mistaken?"

She tittered, then looked to her companions for someone to back her up. A bearded youth stepped over. "This stuff . . ."

"It isn't really us," Vanessa concluded. "My painting has a chance of selling, true enough, because it would go well in the dining room. Does it really interest you, what we're doing?"

"Is that so surprising?"

"Well, I mean . . . a guy like you."

"Just what is that, a guy like me?" I laughed.

"Dunno. You're not exactly easy to please. You don't seem to like young people a whole lot."

"Am I that old?"

"No, but . . . well, I mean, the first time we met you, you were pretty revolting."

"I'd just eaten a godawful lunch that day. But you're right; I am mean. I hate people in general and painters in particular, because they ruin my life. Good or bad, they're always after me. That's what you call a persecution complex.''

I could read on their faces that they were more or less confused as to the real base of my opinions. I made gentle fun of myself.

"I'm an odd duck, eh? You look as though you can't quite get over what I've been telling you. Sure, it's true I'm a cynic, a misanthrope, and a misogynist. As for that, can you name me a single woman painter of genius?''

"Bastard!'' Vanessa Poretski flared.

Seeing my delight, she understood that I'd been hoping for just that.

"You do it on purpose, what's more!''

I smiled as Bruce Conway had taught me, certain of my victory.

"If you want to see a woman painter of genius, here I am,'' she came back at me.

"Prove it!''

Vanessa Poretski lived in the East Village, as one might expect. Beneath the exotic mess of her four-room apartment I could divine some help from home. Her painting studio was of ample proportions. I made a few acid remarks about the source of her revenue, which she didn't appreciate in the least. We had managed to slough off her little friends, which suited us both very well. She showed me a few of her works. Audacious but too complicated, with too many unjustifiably bright colors and a clear lack of technique, yet I found them promising because of the underlying aggressive humor that came through spontaneously.

We exchanged a few more observations before a hush fell between us. Almost like animals, we peered at each other with curiosity, studying every gesture made by the other, ready to bite or scratch. I lashed out abruptly.

"You always wear pants?''

"That bothers you, eh? If I had on a skirt, you could slip your hand up it.''

"I'm not sure I'd want to.''

"Oh, come off it! You want me to believe you're not interested in my cunt!''

I flinched. "I do so hate vulgarity in women!''

"That's obvious. At any rate, you'll never make me believe you came here just to see my paintings.''

54

"Then why did you invite me?"

"I never said I didn't want to screw you."

"Ah! You find me attractive?"

"Hell, no!"

"Then why make love in that case?"

"Because I want to know *how* you screw. That interests me."

"What an odd idea. What part does pleasure play in all this?"

"We'll see."

"Thanks, I don't want you."

"I don't believe you. Anyway, I'm getting undressed, and it would surprise me if you didn't find it pretty tempting after all."

Vanessa peeled off her shirt over her head without bothering to undo the buttons. She had nothing on underneath. I sat on a stool, admiring the view as I smoked. She flung off her shoes with a practiced gesture, unzipped her jeans, tossing them in my direction, and slid her bikini panties down her smooth, round thighs. She turned around several times, running one hand through her hair and fondling her ribs and her breasts with the other. She came to a stop in front of me, her hands linked in front of her.

"I owe you how much for the striptease?" I asked stoically.

"Ten minutes of rapture . . ." she replied, her eyes half-closed.

I took a ten-dollar bill out of my pocket and placed it on the stool I had just vacated. "I don't have the time."

As Vanessa watched, incredulous, I walked toward the door.

"Hey! Come back here, you bastard!"

"I have better things to do than amuse myself with a seventeen-year-old nympho."

"I'm twenty-one, and I'm not—"

"I don't give a damn what you are, but I can certainly tell you what you'll become if you keep on like that."

"You're revolting!"

"Why? Am I the one prostituting myself?"

"You just let me go ahead so you'd get your little thrills, you . . . you . . . pervert!"

Waves of laughter overtook me. I began to find particular charm in Vanessa's body as it trembled with rage.

"You're impotent! Yeah, that's it! A dirty voyeur, a sadist!"

Leaning back against the door, I gazed at her.

By now she seemed bothered, almost embarrassed.

"Why don't you fight back when I insult you?"

"Because what you say is perfectly true. I am a voyeur and sadist. Above all, I'm impotent."

"No!"

"What do you mean, no? It's true. The old machinery just doesn't operate."

"It's not true." She assumed the look of a pouting little girl, more titillating to me than her amateur striptease. Her head dropped in humility, then she shyly asked, "You don't find me attractive?"

"Indeed I do, very much."

Looking up, she came close enough to touch me. Our eyes met in what is called a long and impassioned gaze. Then she rose onto her toes, leaned on my shoulders, and kissed me. It was altogether charming; I was very touched.

"Oh, don't be so mean! What does it take to convince you?"

"Oh, I don't know . . . perhaps to be begged."

"Then I beg you!"

"You beg me what?"

"I beg you to make love to me. I beg you!"

I went home for lunch well satisfied, regretting only that I'd forgotten to take back my ten dollars.

I spent the afternoon polishing my article for James, then gave him a ring. We settled a few things, and finally I promised to go with him the following day to his goddamn Contemporary Arts Day, though I was barely interested.

At seven sharp the hollering on the second floor started up again. I went out on the landing, as did, of course, Colin and Bruce. The latter was accompanied by Sharon Dowd, but to my great relief, Anita did not appear, probably under orders to stay and play in Bruce's apartment.

"They're always at it," I commented.

"Shut up!" Bruce responded. "Listen, what was that she just said?"

"Dick head, I think," offered Colin on his way down to my floor.

As always Beatrice's voice was the easier one to catch,

clearer and more piercing. "Egotist! You're nothing but an egotistic brute! All you want is for me to live somewhere else, to leave you in peace with your sluts and your little orgies! And on top of that, you have the nerve to ask me to pay your rent!"

"You can keep your lousy dough, you whore!"

"Faggot!"

I glanced at Colin.

"That's nothing, I'm used to it," he whispered.

"They're still squabbling over that stupid apartment business," Bruce remarked. "These days they're distinctly short on imagination."

The door on the second floor was yanked open, and Virgil Sparks found himself in the stairway too.

"That's it!" Beatrice shouted. "Go on home, you jerk! And stay there!"

"I've got better fucking things to do than mess around with a petty, hysterical typist!"

Beatrice's red face showed for a moment in the crack of the door. "I'm neither petty, nor hysterical, nor a typist, you flaming asshole!"

Then she slammed the door.

"Ah, women, women!" Virgil bellowed as he climbed the stairs. Looking up, he noticed Bruce and Sharon standing together. "Beware, Bruce! They're witches, women are!"

Without further ado he went inside. Calling down from the fifth floor, Bruce invited us up for a drink. Colin declined on the pretext of work to finish. I could see that his fingers were indeed stained with colored ink. He nodded to me and vanished behind his door. When I reached Bruce Conway's doorway, I found him and Sharon in somewhat of a pickle.

"Anita, unlock the door, sweetie!"

A "No!" came from behind the partition.

"Come on, Anita! Just undo the lock you turned!"

"No!"

"Anita, don't be difficult! You're going to be in *big* trouble!"

"Anita, you're not at home, you little brat!" Bruce raged. "If you don't do as you're told, we'll call the police!"

"I don't care."

"Wait a minute, let me try," I proposed. "Anita, do you hear me?"

"Who's that?"

"I'm the guy you want for a daddy. Do you think I like this? Do you? I certainly don't want to be the daddy of a disobedient little girl. What do you say? You going to let me in or no?"

There was an audible click, and Anita's anxious little face appeared.

"Fine, that's good. If you keep on being good, you'll eventually have a real father."

"You?"

"Or someone else you like a lot."

"Oh, no! Just you!" She turned to Sharon. "Mommy, are you angry?"

"A little."

Finally we went in. The moment I sat down on the sofa, the cat, to my great dismay, settled into my lap. Bruce laughed at my disgruntled expression, and I cursed the demon that had sent me at the same time an adoptive daughter, a repulsive animal, and a misbegotten friend to laugh at my discomfort. Anita got up on the sofa beside me and began staring at me again. While I tried to forget about her, once more her perfume surrounded me, cloaked me, as powerful and intoxicating as the odor of the wild animals in the menageries of touring circuses. Bruce automatically handed me a bourbon. Sharon was sipping at some drink or other while following Bruce's every move. Anita noticed.

"Why are we here, Mommy?"

"We're here visiting our nice friends."

"That one's not my friend." Her stare plainly indicated Bruce.

"Well, in that case he's mine."

"If that's the new daddy, then I don't want him."

"Anita, that's quite enough! I won't stand for any more of your nonsense."

"I don't want him!"

She cuddled up against me, prompting a snarl from Agamemnon.

Bruce, seeming somewhat put off by this contrariness, attempted to cajole the little girl. "Would you like a glass of orange juice, Anita?"

"Don't want it."

"Anita!"

The child must have heard a threat in Sharon's voice, for she kept quiet the rest of the time I was there. I didn't linger long, because this atmosphere, in which a small girl and a cat were contesting the right to poison my life, held no charm for me. Bruce, too, must certainly have been cross at me for deserting him this way, for his farewell was unintelligible.

At last, I was about to cross my own doorstep when a stranger hailed me from the bottom of the stairs.

"Excuse me, but is this where Josh Hardy lives?"

"Yes," I replied. "On the sixth floor."

"What I mean is, mister, you wouldn't want to give me a hand?"

"To do what?"

"Well, to get him home."

I realized then that the man was propping against the wall another individual hidden in the shadows.

"Uh, okay," I mumbled.

Hurrying downstairs, I discovered Josh Hardy in a state of drunkenness that was not simply advanced but rather beyond all limits of human resistance. His degree of inebriation must have been twice the amount considered mortal. What's more, his companion, who strangely resembled him, was holding himself upright with almost equal difficulty. I took pity on him and advised him to go home to bed, promising him several times over that I would manage to get Josh all the way upstairs. Finally he left, weaving and mumbling "Thanks, mister" every three steps. I took hold of Josh as best I could and began the difficult ascent toward the sixth floor. The jolting caused by my burden quickly made me dizzy. I almost went to ask for help but then thought better of it. I accomplished my task as though it were self-punishment for my sins of the day. One floor to go, nine steps to go, seven . . . six, five, four . . . How painful, the path toward the heavens! Three steps before the end, Josh began to talk.

"It's so high up, so high . . ."

Silence. A halt two steps below the summit.

"I'm all the way up . . . can't go any higher . . . see, I can only go down. . . ."

Just one step left to go.

"Here I go . . . I'm falling . . . I'll fall . . . Fall . . ."

I found his keys in the pocket of his jacket and entered the apartment for the first time. It was filthy, dusty, and littered with refuse. I struggled not to breathe so as to keep from gagging.

With some difficulty I got him into bed. He clung frantically to my shoulder, terror suddenly blazing in his eyes that were blinded by the toxic vapors of bad wine. I wondered whether I might not just witness a case of spontaneous combustion.

"No! No!" he cried. "Don't push! He's striking at me again—me, the sinner! Chastised! I'm being chastised . . . down, down . . . the fall . . . darkness . . . damnation!"

Wanting to flee, I stayed rooted to the spot, fascinated yet appalled. Never would I have imagined the least spark of intelligence in Josh Hardy. And here I was, face-to-face with a tortured being, a drunkard who envisioned alcohol as a way to escape a wrathful God. The idea distressed me. Did God wish only to punish? I broke away from his grasp and made a half-turn toward the door.

"Yes . . . the fall . . ."

I closed the door behind me with relief.

Tempted to ring Colin's bell and tell him everything, I decided it would be indecent to divulge the secrets I had just discovered. I was an involuntary witness to be sure, but lucid and responsible.

Could I in any way help Josh Hardy? It was likely that he would forget I had intervened or, at any rate, the things he had revealed. Better that I erase all recollection of his wine-besotted absurdities. Yes, better to return to my private comforts, blot out all thought of others' problems. Just like everyone else, just as always. After all, who holds out a helping hand to me? Why should I help those who do nothing for me?

Blindly reaching for a book on my shelves, I tried to read. Suddenly I realized that I had not had dinner. With a sandwich, a glass of milk, and a container of yogurt brought back from the kitchen, I took up the volume again and opened it to a flyleaf. My eye fell on a line of poetry standing by itself.

"Is there a life before death?"

I let Seamus Heaney's book slip from my hands.

Pausing briefly, then back in motion once more, I went from intellectual immobility to the absolute of materialism. I began to eat.

5. *In which our hero, disabused, makes a discovery and undergoes some disquieting moments*

"Contemporary painting, land of contrasts . . ."

"The gouache with a thousand faces," James Coventry responded in my ear. James and I found ourselves constantly choking back laughter, surprised and delighted by the abundance of clichés pouring from the lecture of the illustrious unknown perched on the rostrum. As promised, I had accompanied James to the Contemporary Arts Day.

I must admit I was not sorry. James was a short, stocky fellow, somewhat bald and myopic, whom I valued highly for his intelligence and his ever-playful humor. We kept on making fun of the speaker, louder than ever, when a cross face looked back in our direction. The auburn curls, the "crushed strawberry" mouth and pretty brown eyes could only belong to Florence Fairchild.

She had recognized me, for she instantly blushed in anger and consternation. James gave me a jab of the elbow.

"Not bad, the young lady down in front."

"Yeah, not too shabby."

"Though she doesn't seem too crazy about our having a few laughs back here in our corner. Perhaps it's her beloved who's addressing us?"

"For her sake I hope not!" I hooted, eyeing the tremor in the orator's triple chin.

"Think it will take him much longer? There's a show in

some of the rooms nearby, and one of my sculptor friends has contributed a piece. You'll see, it's rather neat. Not wildly daring but still good.''

A salvo of frenetic applause indicated that we were not the only ones hoping the address had ended. The occupants of the front rows got to their feet with highly suspect alacrity. Then I found myself face-to-face with Ms. Fairchild.

''Mr. Tuncurry,'' she began. ''Flavius's advanced years do not give you leave to openly insult him. He has done a great deal for art in his day, and the least one can offer him is a bit of respect.''

''You're just exactly who again?'' I asked with a yawn.

She must have been prepared for anything but that, the idea that I might have forgotten her being utterly inconceivable.

''Florence Fairchild,'' she stated coldly. ''And Flavius is my uncle.''

''Ms. Fairchild, I couldn't care less whether that old crock is your husband or your grandfather or your lover. I only ask that he not make a public nuisance of himself.''

James was following the whole thing with immense pleasure, hoping I'd get a slap in the face or a chair across the top of my head. Florence Fairchild stiffened and clenched her fists, trying desperately not to lose her composure, a feat I denied her. After a second yawn I went on.

''Ah, yes, Fairchild . . . now I remember. How could I have forgotten a woman with such breasts?''

The smile on James's face froze, and his eyes turned back to my victim. Her response was brief. She struck my face with the back of her hand, her ring grazing the corner of my mouth and tearing the skin. Instinctively I touched the painful spot and discovered that I was bleeding profusely.

''You're simply despicable,'' she hissed with an ugly sneer.

She turned on her heels and went off. People were eyeing me strangely, and a few stopped in their tracks. Pressing my handkerchief to my mouth, I headed for the rest rooms, escorted by James, who wanted to know all about Ms. Fairchild. I complacently told him what I knew as I checked the damage in the mirror. I had a splendid cut on the left side. We waited in the men's room for the blood to stop flowing. After ten minutes it did.

''Come on,'' said James, leading the way. ''We'll go see the sculpture. It's this way. No, that way.''

We found ourselves in something resembling a railway station waiting room filled with gadgets. I was instantly put off, particularly when my eye fell upon a bicycle wheel.

"Oh, no, not that!" I groaned.

James laughed. "Come on. Let's keep looking. My buddy is around here somewhere."

"I'd rather go back to the men's room."

Taking me by the arm, James forced me to follow. Soon we were quite lost.

"Wait a sec . . . I don't get it," he was saying. "It's got to be here."

"Perhaps he's in another gallery," I suggested, full of hope, after gazing dejectedly at a jam jar placed on a pressure cooker.

"Gorgeous art object," he responded, noting my disgusted expression. "Okay, suppose we try the other direction?"

I held him back by the sleeve. Between a chair painted green and a pink radiator, I had just caught sight of Florence Fairchild in deep discussion with a young couple. We sneaked behind a Venus de Milo rising from a pile of garbage to listen unobserved.

"Repetitive music," the lovely Florence was saying, "really puts me in a hypnotic state. Steve Reich, for instance, fascinates me. . . ."

I left my hiding place so abruptly that I caused all three of them to start. I didn't leave them time to recover.

"Thus, Ms. Fairchild, you classify Steve Reich under the rubric of 'repetitive music.' Well, I do not altogether agree. Reich does eliminate certain aspects of discourse—harmony or melody, for instance—and works on progressions of density and rhythm, which produce counteracting phenomena of a harmonic or melodic nature. In that sense I believe one could say Steve Reich is not a 'repetitive' but rather an 'evolutionary' musician. How do you feel about that?"

"Is there any field in which you do not pretend to hold absolute knowledge, Mr. Tuncurry?" she retorted.

"Yes, indeed. I know nothing about doing laundry."

"You know what? You are a consummate, irremediable jerk."

"I have no doubt about that, but how do you find my analysis of Steve Reich?"

"I don't wish to talk to you."

"Oh, is that so? In that case you admit defeat?"

"I do not do battle, and consequently, I have no reason

whatsoever to consider myself defeated. I simply want to be rid of you. You're so precisely everything I detest that you're almost a caricature of it.''

''I believe you have a totally mistaken view of Foster,'' James remarked. ''He shows whichever side of himself he pleases. Right at the moment he wants to be hateful, but he can just as well be sweetness personified. Contrary to what you think, he is an intelligent person.''

''In that case, it's still worse.''

''It is worse,'' I agreed. ''It's very kind of you, James, but I need no defense. If I am just what you hate, Ms. Fairchild, then the feeling is reciprocal. I abhor haughty young women who look upon others with scorn and false assumptions, pretending to be well brought-up and proper, while they are nothing more than hypocrites. I abhor middle-class women who go into ecstasy and cry genius over red or blue blobs, and I've always abhorred the girls in public relations who have relations but nothing to do with the public. You waste praise that should go to the artists whom you ignore, dazzled as you are by Schmidt's forgers and the senile drivelings of your great-great-uncle. You don't do battle? Too bad. I declare war. War against all the Sigmund Schmidts, all profiteers. Against all who hold the pursestrings and the power. Art shouldn't be for profit! But the artist has to live. Yet how many die because of the failures and exploiters always in their way? How many give up because it's that or die? Yes, I'm hateful! Yes, I'm nasty! So much the better. But at least I remain unsullied!''

I came to a halt, breathless. A moment of silence ensued. A few people had gathered around us to hear my tirade.

''You should do me an article,'' James finally blurted.

''Another?''

I managed to catch the furtive eye of Florence Fairchild, who was biting her lip. She didn't try to respond. There was actually nothing to say. She slowly walked away without raising her head. The ring of rubberneckers was quick to break up because, in the end, there was nothing to see. I stayed there alone with James.

''Hey, now,'' he said, ''we're right in front of my buddy's sculptures. Look here, I didn't even see them.''

''What's your buddy's name?''

''Blue Cloud.''

''Eh?''

"Well, yes. He's a Navajo."

"In fact, there is something of the totem about them."

"You bet; absolutely. He describes them as mystic woods."

"Why not?"

"Right. Not bad, is it?"

"Yup, it's bearable. You should suggest that he screw in some sixty-watt bulbs."

"You're exaggerating!" James guffawed. "This is a whole lot better than a supermarket standing lamp."

"Well, now, aside from this warehouse of symbolic objects, do you suppose there's anything else of interest around here?"

"Actually, there is a show by one painter."

"Let's try the painter, and we'll see."

"It's in room fifteen on the next floor."

He tugged at my sleeve, conscientiously guiding me toward the stairs. I prayed to heaven it wouldn't be green squares and yellow triangles.

Room fifteen wasn't very large, and aside from the canvases, it was empty.

"Well, well," I whispered, "it's not exactly packed."

"No. They're all downstairs where they'll be seen. You know as well as I that art is only a pretext in this sort of event."

"Careful, James! You're getting to be as cynical as I am!"

Then I went up to the paintings.

"Terrific," James began. He broke off abruptly. "Now this is really something," he went on. Then he came to a stop again. "Do you see what I see?" he asked.

"I don't know. What do you see?"

"Shit! This is fabulous work!"

We moved to the next painting, a small, pink watercolor representing a carnation. But there, too, the petals concealed strange creations. The third work was half painting, half sculpture, everything in motion, in hollows and relief. The fourth was woven, a sort of abstract medieval tapestry from which hung a wooden harlequin worked into the geometric composition with art and skill.

We stood there a good while in mute admiration, going hot and cold, at the very least surprised.

"Who did them?" James murmured, clearing his throat.

"It must say someplace. Wait. There. Grindling Conrad Exhibition. Don't know him."

"Me neither. But I swear I'll make him known."

"Okay," I said. "We'll join in a campaign to promote an unknown artist?"

"Anytime you like, buddy! We'll have to find someone from the gallery who can fill us in. There's a good chance these days that what's-his-name Conrad is part of the establishment. We'll have to get our hands on him. What is his name again? Grindling? What an idea!"

We went back down with restored enthusiasm and ardor. For a while we wandered through electric blue corridors and rooms mottled with people, but when we reached the reception desk, nobody was there.

"Could have bet on it," James grumbled.

I sat down nonchalantly in the empty chair and crossed my feet on the desk. An elderly couple came up to us.

"Excuse me," said the man. "Could you tell us where the HIBC is meeting?"

"Of course, sir," I replied cheerily. "It's on the sixth floor, Room 607."

"I'm much obliged, young man." We watched them walk away.

"What do you suppose it is, the HIBC?" asked James.

"No idea whatsoever."

"That was a pretty lousy trick, you know. Poor people!"

"If they don't like it, they can complain to the management."

A woman in a hideous flowered dress was barreling down the corridor toward us. "What are you doing there?" she shouted when still thirty feet away.

Her voice irritated me. I made no reply but began to rock back and forth with my feet still on the desk.

"Up, up! Out of there!"

She finally reached us. I didn't budge. With a quiver of her lower lip she went on.

"Get up, that is my place."

"Do you have proof of your claim?"

"What?" she stood gaping.

Stifling his laughter, James asked, "We would like some information about the Grindling Conrad Exhibition."

"Second floor, room fifteen."

"Yes, that much we know. But we would like to meet Mr. Conrad."

"In that case I cannot help you."

"And do you know where we might find Mr. Spenser?"

"Never heard of him."

"But . . . he's one of the organizers of the Contemporary Arts Day."

"I do not know him. Would you kindly return my chair?"

"You are so polite that I cannot refuse." I stood up, inadvertently turning over both the seat and the telephone. "Oh, sorry!"

We reluctantly decided to leave. Suddenly, on our way out the main exit, James grew animated. He bounded forward, saying, "There we are! Follow me."

After jostling a few worthy citizens we caught up with the aforementioned Spenser.

"Hello, Spenser!"

"Well, it's James Coventry. How're things going, my friend?"

"Fine, thanks. I'd like you to meet Foster Tuncurry."

"Delighted."

I replied with a nod.

"Look here, Spenser. We've just seen the Grindling Conrad exhibit, and we'd like to meet the guy. That possible?"

Spenser pursed his lips.

"Conrad. You know, this is the first and last time I undertake anything for him. He's so disagreeable. You have no idea!"

"Oh, I see." James glanced at me.

"Even if he's unbearable, his painting makes it worth the trial of putting up with him," I noted.

He shrugged. "I'm not exactly fanatic about him."

"Doesn't matter," I insisted. "The guy must have some address."

"Yeah. Have to look it up in my papers."

"Good, could you do it now?" I was almost pleading.

"Afraid not. The stuff is in my office, not here."

What frustration!

He addressed James. "What if I give you a ring tomorrow?"

"Fine," James said. "I'll be expecting it."

"At any rate, if you should ever happen to run into Grindling Conrad, there'll be no mistaking him. He's at least six-two with red hair, incredible eyes, and apparel that would bowl you over. And the minute he opens his mouth, it's to work you over or bring you down in flames. Be forewarned! Well, if you'll excuse me now, I've got to run. Don't worry, James. I'll give you a buzz tomorrow.''

We watched him go off. ''What do you make of all that?''

''That Spenser is an idiot.''

''Yes, but what else? He sounds like an odd one, this Conrad, no?''

''I suppose it goes with his painting.''

''Hmm . . . guess so. Well, we'll see.''

''You have anything more to do in this joint?''

''Yes. I'm going to try to catch Blue Cloud. You staying?''

''No, I've had it. You'll let me know about Conrad?''

''Yes, don't worry. The minute I get the lowdown, I'll call. Then we'll decide what we can do, okay?''

''Okay. 'Bye, James.''

''So long.''

I treated myself to a taxi ride home.

In my mind I began an article on Grindling Conrad. I had reworked my opening sentence thirty-two times before the cab pulled up at the door of my building. All at once an idea dawned on me. Here I was living in Stairway C, and yet I knew nothing about either Stairway A or B. I had a sudden desire to see them. Stairway A was to the left, off the entry walk from the street. Climbing the first few steps, I craned to look at the upper floors. There was no apparent difference. Stairway B was at the center of the entry court. I repeated my experiment and came to the same conclusions. Finally I started up my own Stairway C to the right, all but discouraged to see that it was exactly like the others. A stairway is never more than steps and a railing. As I was slowly and sadly climbing the first flight, an enthusiastic hello and a clatter of footsteps announced the bounding presence of Bruce Conway behind me. I knew then that there was really only one Stairway C. Bruce tapped me on the shoulder.

''Well, friend, how's life?''

''Fine. You seem to be on top of the world.''

''In a way, in a way.''

His eyes were darting all around as he jumped up and down in place. He was even more hyper than usual.

"What's up?"

"Me? Nothing. Perhaps I've finally hit on a job. Well, I mean, I'll know by tomorrow."

"You don't mean it! What sort of work?"

"Oh, just a job, you know . . ."

"Aha!"

"I wanted to ask you, uh . . ."

"For money, as usual?"

"Yes . . . uh, I mean, no. This time, if I've got the job, I can pay you back. But I might need something to tide me over. It's mostly that I owe cash to some guys who'd be real happy to get it back. Aside from that, um . . . what do you think of Sharon Dowd?"

I snickered at the *non sequitur*. "That her daughter is unnerving."

"Right, but what about *her?*"

"What do you want me to say? She looks like a loser: unreliable, a bit gullible."

"Oh, I see."

I could tell by his suddenly glum expression that this was not the kind of response he'd been hoping to get.

"Why is my view of Sharon of any interest to you?"

"No reason. Just asking."

"You in love?"

"Me?"

He assumed an offended expression that reassured me. Then he blushed, which alarmed me.

"I'm a liar," he added, frowning. He roared with laughter. "Nobody lies like Bruce Conway! Well, then, yes! I *am* in love! So what? Is it serious, Doc?"

"It is a serious matter if you fall for a girl like Sharon Dowd."

"You get my goat, Foster."

"That may be, but if you let her get her hooks into you, you won't find it easy to shake her off. And don't forget the charming Anita. Come to think of it, who *is* her daddy?"

"You're not very nice, Foster."

"It's quite clear that *nice* has never been my dominant trait."

"I think you're mistaken about Sharon. She hasn't had much luck up to now and—"

"What's more, she's going to put a jinx on you! See? It's al-

ready begun. You've already found work. Where will all the
calamities lead to if you go on seeing her?''

He threw me a look I didn't like one bit. ''You don't know
what you're saying. If I've got this job, it's *because* of her.''

''What do you mean?''

''That I'm not going to play the clown all my life. I'm getting on, you know, and I've no intention of winding up alone.
There are times when you've got to make a choice. That's what
I'm in the process of doing. Believe me, old man, death comes
sooner than you think.''

''Drop the morbidity. It doesn't suit you in the least.''

''Oh, every now and then I'm serious.''

''Well, cut it out, because I don't like it. You're only bearable when you're raving.''

''I don't give a damn what you like. And you get on my
nerves.'' He went up a few steps and glanced back. ''You don't
call all the shots, after all.''

''What kind of a job is it?''

''Stockroom boy.''

''What?''

''You heard me.''

''You're not really going to take a job like that, are you?''

''Yes, I am. And even if I cringed at the thought, I'd do it
just to bug you!''

Then he took the stairs at full speed.

''I'm not through! Bruce, come back here!''

''Go to hell!''

I heard him slam his door. For a moment I stood rooted
there, abashed, unable to collect my wits. And then I thought of
Colin Shepherd. I wanted to talk to him. But I knew he wasn't
home yet, and I was sure he would find me at fault. Even if he
were desperately in love with Bruce, he would do nothing to
dissuade him from living with Sharon. I was alone in wanting
and being able to combat this miserable stroke of luck. However, I refused to ask myself why I was overcome with such
fury, why I was so disturbed by it. I finally decided to pursue
Bruce all the way to his apartment. I had to ring several times
before getting any answer.

''Who is it?''

''It's me. Open up, will you?''

''Can't. I'm taking a shower.''

"Bruce!"

Not a word.

"Bruce!"

"Leave me alone! I've got nothing on, the water's running. Besides, I'm sick of you!"

"Bruce, listen! Bruce!"

I pounded on the door. Then it occurred to me how fruitless my efforts were. I could do nothing but hope that all this would blow over during the night. For I firmly intended to continue with the offensive the next day. As I went back down toward the third floor I was suddenly aware of a hush. Supposedly silence is a prelude to revelation. I found that thought amusing. The revelation would be for Bruce Conway, when I had made him see reason. Oddly, it never dawned on me that I might be more directly concerned.

When I reached my floor, I leaned back against the wall and breathed deeply. The lights went out. The fuse must have gone again, I mused, and the landlord still hadn't done the promised rewiring. Unconcerned about that, I grabbed the railing with both hands and gripped very hard, until I no longer felt the pressure on my palms. Then I leaned out across the stairwell and gradually looked toward the upper floors.

The dim light, the smell of damp plaster and floor wash, the numbness in my fingers and the zigzag of the staircase combined to make me dizzy. A wide bank of shadow crossed the fifth floor, and the sixth was almost invisible. Only a single streak darker than the rest suggested the presence of something beyond.

The blood was throbbing in my temples, and everything went blurry. It seemed to me that the dark shadow way up there was beating in time with my own heart, swinging in space. I lunged backward and staggered for an instant, terrified.

I leaned against my door, my cheek rubbing the wood. Its warmth and solidity calmed me. Nevertheless it took me an eternity of ponderous seconds before I could shake off my sense of alarm. The lights came back on, and I looked for my keys. I didn't have them. I could remember taking them out while talking with Bruce. Luckily I spotted the keys on the steps where I had dropped them without noticing. As I toyed with them for a moment the cool metal allayed the last vestiges of my panic. I went into my apartment where my feeling of security could not entirely block out a sort of regret at leaving Stairway C.

I was disturbed by its force, little short of magnetic, the feeling of possession that emanated from it. Within its silence, Stairway C had seized me, had shown me a certain strangeness that I couldn't understand. Unwittingly I had been initiated, but the Mystery was still concealed from me.

At that point in my reflections I heard a scratching. I thought that Agamemnon was trying to get in, and for once I was ready to welcome his warm presence. But it was not the cat.

"Can I come in, Daddy?"

I looked at Anita without reacting, then shook myself. "What are you doing here? Are you alone?"

"Yes. Can I come and play here?"

"Do you know what time it is? Where's your mother?"

She tilted her head in a way that said "up there."

"She's at Bruce Conway's. Is that right?"

"Yes."

I had a strong desire to send her away but didn't dare. "Why aren't you with them?"

"Mommy told me to go home. I'm not going." She crossed her arms, pouting. There was not a thing I could do.

"You know, Anita, there's nothing to play with here."

"Doesn't matter."

She sat down on my sofa, her hands between her knees. Obviously she wasn't going to budge.

"Like something to drink?"

"No."

"You can clearly see that there's nothing here to interest you. Why don't you go home instead and play with all your toys?"

"No."

"You'll be bored, you know."

"That doesn't matter, Daddy."

"Anita, please! Don't call me that again!"

She first seemed very sad, then angry. "I wanted to tell you a secret."

"What?"

"Mommy is going to live with the other daddy. But I don't want to. What're you going to do about it?"

"What do you mean? Why, nothing at all!"

It struck me that Anita and I had virtually the same intentions. After all, she was quite capable of pestering them to the point where they'd give up the idea of communal life.

"I want to come here. Where can I sleep?"

"But Anita, I . . . it's out of the question for you to sleep here."

I could read the disappointment on her face.

"It's not fair! Everyone is mean to me." She began to cry with application and know-how.

Suddenly her shrieks echoed up and down the stairs. I opened the door to find myself face-to-face with Sharon Dowd.

For an instant we stared at each other without speaking, until the sobbing caught the mother's ear.

"Anita? Why . . . what on earth are you doing in Mr. Tuncurry's apartment? You're crying?"

Sharon turned to me angrily. "What have you done to her?"

"Why, nothing at all. Your daughter came to me seeking sanctuary. I couldn't leave her in a deserted hallway."

"Come along, Anita, we're going home."

"No! I'm staying with my daddy."

Sharon grabbed her daughter by the arm and dragged her out the door, closing it behind them without a word. I was alone again and, on the whole, relieved to be rid of Anita.

I lingered with my eyes closed, letting myself slip into daydreams. I was beginning to drift off when the sound of voices raised in anger let me know that Virgil and his beloved Beatrice were back. I bent an ear, trying to catch it. The words melded into a sort of incantation, a melody that went up and down the scales irregularly. There were sudden crescendos with accents fortissimo, followed by a moment or two of andante allegro, until the whole thing turned to cacophony. They were off again for another bout. I felt neither the patience nor the equanimity to endure a new domestic wrangle. Fuming to myself, I got to my feet and went to ring Virgil's door bell. It was a good three minutes before they came to open up. Virgil made a great show of pleasure, clearly happy that I had come to interrupt their dispute.

"You really show no pity at all for your neighbors," I said.

"I thought we were the building's principal attraction," snapped Beatrice, apparently little disposed to being agreeable.

Virgil glanced my way with a raised eyebrow as though to say, "You see what I have to put up with, my friend?"

"What's up this time?" I inquired.

"The same as always," she said.

"The two apartments?"

"Exactly."

"Seems idiotic, eh?" Beatrice added.

I hesitated to sit down, for the atmosphere was hardly clement.

"Would you like a drop of something?" Virgil offered.

I accepted, settling into an armchair. I broached a new topic.

"You know that Bruce has found a job and that he intends to live with Sharon Dowd?"

"He's mad!" Virgil exclaimed.

"That's what he used to be. But he's turning grave and well organized, and that's *really* serious."

"The job, that's not so bad. . . ." Virgil went on with his theme. "But for him to adopt domestic life!"

"That's just what I think. Let's hope he'll have changed his mind in a couple of days. With him that's perfectly possible."

"Why that 'let's hope'?" Beatrice wanted to know. "Just because he's Bruce Conway, he has no right to live with the woman of his choice? Your petty judgments are perfectly revolting."

"Staying single and free, Tuncurry," Sparks commented, "is the only way to keep the peace. Come to think of it, Colin Shepherd is the luckiest of all. He at least doesn't clutter up his place with female pests."

"You can just let me know when you're through with your stinking male chauvinist discussion," Beatrice rejoined as she got to her feet. "Meanwhile the pest will go get the crackers and cheese the boor forgot to put out."

"Lighten up!" Virgil remarked with the trace of a smile as she stalked into the kitchen. "She's actually not all that angry."

When I left Virgil's apartment, he and his dearly beloved were temporarily reconciled. That's the way it always went. Perhaps for once I would have a calm, quiet evening. I was all primed for my article on Grindling Conrad. I began, I stopped, I began again. Finally I gave up for the time being and went down for my mail, which I had neglected to do for two days.

I stepped outdoors to throw all the junk mail into the trash. There was also a letter from my father. Leaning back against the bank of mailboxes, I read the opening, "My dear, unworthy son . . ."

The lights went out. Someday I'd really have to raise a row with the super about that. I sighed, and they flickered back on again.

But in the interim I felt chills run up my spine. During the few seconds of darkness some creature had appeared in the entrance doorway. It had all happened so rapidly, so unexpectedly, that I stood there rooted with fear before this apparition dressed all in black—and so black itself. Then I recognized Mrs. Bernhardt.

"Oh, hello," I said, clearing my throat. "You surprised me. I didn't hear you come in."

I managed to give her a smile. She had not moved an inch but stared at me out of the dark pupils all but hidden by the yellow wrinkles of her eyelids. This first time our eyes met I saw the tears moistening her lashes. Slowly turning her head away, she moved toward the stairs. Gripping the railing with bony fingers, she went up two steps and stopped, her face toward the ground. Her lips trembled, and I knew she was about to speak to me.

"I would like to have died in Jerusalem," she said.

I tried to think of some reply, something to comfort her. I failed. I watched her slow ascent to her apartment. I hadn't done a thing.

I hadn't done a thing.

Colin Shepherd's words came back to me: "The worst part of it is that she doesn't rebel." Mrs. Bernhardt was about to prove him wrong; I was sure of it. Yes, she was going to rebel against her fate; she was going to fight.

Then, once again, I saw her face and form, just as they had been suddenly revealed to me. I trembled. Something moist ran down my chin, and I raised a hand to my mouth. I was bleeding. Without realizing it I had bitten my lip to the point of drawing blood.

6.

"Thus the evanescent form will let
The soul, released at last,
Ascend towards
The myriad stars . . ."

> —*Aux bords du fleuve sacré* (On
> the Banks of the Sacred River)
> by M.D. Calvocoressi; set to
> music by A. Roussel in *Evo-*
> *cations.*

For the fifty-third time I dealt out a game of solitaire. When it didn't come out, I put away the cards. I tried to concentrate on something but couldn't accomplish a thing. In desperation I picked up a novel and got into bed. By four in the morning I had finished the book and still couldn't sleep. I resigned myself to taking a sleeping pill. At six I was awake, at seven I was dozing. At eight the phone rang. I refused to answer. Finally, at nine o'clock there was nothing to do but get up.

That's what you call starting the day well.

It was too early to go up and see Bruce, so I killed time by concocting a most thoroughly pontifical, moralizing speech in my head. Roughly it would lean on Blake's credo that "opposition is true friendship." After imagining Bruce's response, I turned to something else.

There was the option of going up for breakfast with Colin, but I decided not to talk to him until I had settled the Bruce Conway problem. To tell the truth, I was so sure of his reaction that I feared losing my resolve and determination at first sight of

75

him. But I had to succeed. Yet I regretted not being able to tell him about my encounter with Mrs. Bernhardt. There were still terrible, unreal images before my eyes, and Colin alone would understand me. Recalling my agitation and anguish of the previous evening, I trembled and spilled a bit of coffee. I simply couldn't find an explanation for what had happened to me.

Faint strains of music were drifting down from Colin's place: Bach. I resisted calling for help. No, I wouldn't go up.

A door slammed. Virgil or Beatrice had just left. Given the hour, I suspected it was Beatrice.

A bit later I heard Colin's footsteps. Bending an ear, I waited for him to creak the floorboards of my landing. When he paused in front of my door I smiled. Then he continued on his way.

Knowing the futility of waking Bruce in the early hours, I attempted to spend the morning on intelligent pursuits. Accordingly, I called James Coventry. "Did you get anything on Conrad?" I asked him.

"Yup. Spenser slipped me his address. At least we can grant him that much—the guy generally does as he promises. But, look here, what's-his-name . . ."

"Grindling Conrad."

"Yeah, Grindling Conrad. He has no phone. We'll have to root him out."

"Can you do it today?" I asked.

"By myself?"

"For the first contact. After that I'll take over, I swear."

"Okay, will do. . . . Look here, Spenser mentioned all over again that he's an odd bird, you know. I must admit that I'm dreading the encounter. The way he tells it, he has some Viking forbears, an Irish grandmother at the very least. Look here, with your evil genius pitted against his, it ought to be interesting."

"We'll see. So you'll call me back, eh?"

"Sure, don't worry."

"So long."

"Farewell."

I hung up, well satisfied. I had just ducked a real chore.

As I was about to get dressed I glanced at myself in the mirror. There were bluish circles under my eyes and hollows in my cheeks. In the midst of my emaciated face, my eyes gleamed with a curious light. I paused in front of the mirror, trying to define my expression. I could have been taken for a dying man, feverish and haggard. But that wasn't it. A madman, rather, or one possessed. No, not that either. . . . The exact description came to me suddenly: I looked evil, uncivilized. The essential thing was missing from my eyes—the focus. Was I still myself?

I shrugged and walked to the bathroom, where I managed to give myself an almost human appearance. I had taken care to put on blue jeans, so as to be on the same wavelength as Bruce. A bit before noon I went upstairs.

Bruce opened the door and looked me up and down. Seeing him in a gray suit, I realized I'd taken the wrong tack. We wouldn't be on the same level.

"In what frame of mind have you come?" he asked.

"Serious, frank, and friendly," I replied, forcing a smile.

I quickly choked back the desire to give him Blake's thing about opposition being true friendship. It was no time for joking.

"This is starting poorly."

"Oh, please, Bruce—"

"Very well. Would you, um . . . be so kind as to enter?" He stepped aside and bowed facetiously. "I note, Mr. Tuncurry, that the uniform of the day is distinctly informal. . . ."

"Hey, cut it out, will you?"

"Easy to see that someone around here isn't in the mood for laughter today."

I sat down on the sofa, and after studying my hands, I said, "You're already dressed?"

"Yes. I've just come in, actually."

I was surprised not to have heard him. I must have been in the shower at that moment.

"And what were you doing up and out at dawn?" I inquired.

"I went to see my personnel director. I'm starting work on Monday."

Astonished, I watched him going around in circles.

"You don't mean it!" I finally said.

"You bet. Warehouseman in a light-bulb factory . . . out on Long Island. I'll have to give some thought to joining the union."

"Well, I mean, Bruce, you can't be serious. You're simply

not going to live with that ninny, heave cartons for pennies, and shelter that pest Anita?''

He came to a halt and stood staring at me.

"Not you . . . you . . . Free as the air," I went on. "The anarchist, the madman . . . I can't let you do it."

"Who are you? My father? My brother? My legal guardian?"

"I have the right and the duty to protect you against—"

"Right? Duty?"

I stood up, furious. "Exactly! The duty . . . and the right to tell you what I think. Sharon is a gold digger and a whore on the make!"

Bruce Conway struck me in the face.

"You're a miserable shit, Tuncurry! You're selfish and mean! You only like to destroy things!"

I wanted to shriek, wanted to strangle him, but I merely sobbed, "Oh, please, Bruce."

I broke off, feeling close to tears. The whole thing was complicated. I was suddenly aware of how much I depended on him. I thought of Colin and Hal. To a degree we had duplicated their scenario. Bruce had used me, used my money. And how many times had he cuffed me, even socked me hard, a thing I'd have taken from no one else?

Unashamed, I let the tears roll down my cheeks. He looked at me calmly. "I'll be damned! Is this a display of jealousy?"

"You owe me a pile of dough, and you'd better give it back on the double," I said with a gasp.

"It's so comforting to know one can count on one's friends!"

"You can drown, for all I care. Anyway, you and she won't last two months together."

"We'll see. In the meantime I owe money all over the place. I'll need at least a thousand. Are you going to give it to me?"

"Yes. Provided you swear to drop Sharon."

"Are you trying to buy me?"

"Does that shock you? You *are* up for sale, aren't you?"

"I suggest we end this stupid argument right there. And, incidentally, if you don't give a shit whether I die, why are you crying?"

"You hit me hard. It hurt."

"No kidding? So it's necessary to hit you to extract the least bit of feeling?"

I bit my lip. "Right," I said. "A feeling of pain. That's all you've gotten out of me."

"It's a good start. When you've really suffered, perhaps you'll be capable of love."

"Because now I'm not?"

"Apparently. Malice, jealousy, possessiveness . . . hardly traits of the perfect lover."

"You're in no position to lecture me on that."

"Why so?"

I turned my back without replying.

"I pity you, Foster."

I did an immediate about-face. "And just who do you think you are? So now you pity me! Is that so? In a couple of weeks we'll see who needs consoling."

I strode across the room. "And above all," I added, reaching for the door handle, "don't forget to sign up with the union."

Tempting though it was, I avoided slamming the door. Calm. I'd stay calm. I had started slowly on my way down when I realized that someone else was on the stairs. I leaned out slightly across the banister and stood still, waiting. A hand was sliding up the railing. At the turn between the fourth and fifth floors Sharon Dowd appeared. On catching sight of me, she was startled. But she instantly recovered and, drawing herself up proudly, continued on up the stairs. "Hello, Mr. Tuncurry," she said as she passed me. "Lovely day, isn't it?"

I could hear the tone of irony in her voice. Bristling, I decided to attack.

"Hello, Miss Dowd. A lovely day indeed. For predators."

"Predators?" She looked down at me from three steps above. "First off, I needn't account to you. Second, I don't give a damn what you think. And, finally . . ."

"Finally?"

"There's nothing you can do about it. Bruce Conway is mine. And you'll never get him."

"I find your views rather disturbing, and I doubt they would please Bruce."

"Go tell him yourself, in that case."

"I could, but I don't have the time to waste."

"Is that so? You haven't just come from there, by any chance?"

"Me? Ah, yes, quite true. I went to ask for the money he owes me. He doesn't have it. Are you paying up for him?"

"That's his problem, not mine."

"Oh, I see. I suppose you'll live under the principle of separate means. Otherwise you'd be obliged to pay his debts. His creditors are beginning to turn ugly, you know. . . . As you'll soon see, Bruce throws money out the window. Bruce has always had a knack for finding friends to lean on. Seduction is his thing. Just look at the way he pitched in the moment he laid eyes on you. Remember?"

I waited for her to reply. Disconcerted, she let her jaw drop. My ploy was succeeding.

"I don't believe you. . . ."

"Oh, pay no attention to me. . . . I simply want my bundle back. Well, I'm off." I waved, flashing a broad grin. "Goodbye, my friend."

I went downstairs, feeling pleased. She quickly climbed the steps, and I heard the sound of keys, then Bruce's voice, clear though muffled. "That you, Sharon?"

To my great surprise I found Colin Shepherd leaning against the wall beside my door. His arms were crossed, and on seeing me, he frowned.

"Well, now, what're you doing there?"

"Waiting for you," he replied.

"Been there for long?"

"Long enough."

A shiver caught me between the shoulder blades. Blow for blow, he had taken in my exchange with Sharon. I soon had the confirmation.

"You get a kick out of that?" he asked.

"What?"

"News travels fast around this place, Foster. Bruce already told me about your argument yesterday. From what I just overheard, it's going from bad to worse. Might I ask what's gotten into you?"

"She's a bitch. Bruce let himself be taken in, that's clear. You'd do better to help me rather than sermonize."

"That's right, Foster. I am going to help you."

"You are?"

That surprised me. Colin's tone and the look on his face were very unfamiliar, and I couldn't quite picture what was going through his head.

"Yes, I'll help you. But not the way you think. Come on, we're going to my place."

"Why to your place?"

"Don't argue. Come along."

I hesitated, wondering what Colin must think of my behavior.

"You coming?" His impatient tone completely unnerved me. I could only follow him. We went into his apartment without a word. Colin shut and locked the door behind us. This was growing more peculiar by the moment.

"Sit down."

With a lump in my throat I obeyed. Colin took a stand in front of me and observed me intently for several seconds.

"Foster," he began, "I've often fought down the idea that you were fundamentally and instinctively bad. Today, to my great sorrow, I have to admit the truth in what Bruce Conway has always claimed about you. You're mean-spirited."

"Because I say what I think? I call that being frank."

"That never excused anybody."

"Excused? You're off your rocker. As if I were trying to justify myself! Sure, I'm mean-spirited. It's true! I was born of Lucifer, the Archangel of Light. It's innate, you're right. Yes, I do want to hurt! I love to see people crumple before my will! You know what I like best of all? To dominate others, to let them know they're my inferiors! To be on top is worth nothing unless others realize they're underneath!"

I paused to catch my breath, hoping he would stop me before I reached my threshold of vulnerability. But he waited for me to finish.

"You're nothing but a dirty little fag! D'you realize how I abominate you?"

Beneath the tensing muscles of his face, I could see the jutting jaw. He squinted, continuing to stare me down without blinking. I stood up and stepped forward. I was a good bit taller than he and much stronger.

"What'll you do if I hit you?"

"Go right ahead."

"I always knew you liked that. . . ."

"Clearly."

"I know what you're going to say."

"Oh, really?"

"Yes, you're going to say that you pity me. Like that cretin, Hal."

"You've never inspired my pity. But you'll wind up provoking my anger."

"So much the better! That'll make one more customer for Satan."

"I've been damned a long time running."

"That's for sure. At what age did you get interested in your little pals? Eh? During adolescence? Of course. What was the name of the first one you buggered? He was younger than you? Perhaps you forced him?"

He brushed a lock of hair from his forehead with a steady hand. "Go on, Foster. Spit it all out. I'd rather it were on me than on Bruce or Sharon. See, I've taken a whole lot more than you could ever lay on me. I can stand your abuse."

"And if I really paste you one? That would hurt you, wouldn't it?"

"Of course. So go ahead. Hit me. Hit me!"

I clenched my left fist and brought it up level with his lips. "That's what you want, you bitch!"

"Yes, you're right."

I was incapable of touching him and I knew it.

"Why do you take this?" I asked.

"I told you why, but you don't understand. I'm helping you."

"Wha?"

"You're a drowning man, and you're struggling against the person who wants to help save you. When you've overcome your fear, you'll be able to swim to shore."

"Fear? Fear of what?"

"Of loving."

I burst out laughing. "That takes the cake!"

"Yeah, funny, isn't it?"

I tried to keep on laughing. Actually I was in full hysteria. I buried my face in my hands, panting for a moment, then sobbing, seeking the oxygen that was eluding me.

"What's happening to you?" Colin's anxious voice came to me from a great distance.

My hysteria was taking over. Hardly conscious, I relied on

the automatic responses I'd had since childhood. "A plastic bag . . . I need . . ." I managed to gasp.

For years I hadn't had one of these spasms. Violent emotion, panic, had revived my old nemesis.

"What? What for? What should I do?"

"Carbon dioxide . . ."

After holding on as long as I could, I slumped and gave in altogether, finally happy to escape the real world. Colin must have understood, for I came around quickly. Brushing away the bag, I breathed almost normally once more. I drew my feet up onto the sofa and flopped out flat. Now that he was no longer worried about my health, Colin began to smile. I read on his face that curious expression of victory I'd seen hints of earlier. To get even I tried to make him feel guilty.

"Pleased? You've managed to make me sick."

"So it's my fault?"

Apparently he wouldn't let himself be taken in that easily. I put some effort into appearing deathly ill, which wasn't too difficult, given that I'd been nursing a terrible headache since the day before, anyway.

"Do you need a doctor?"

"Why? It's over for now."

"Then you're okay?"

"No, not at all."

I shut my burning eyes. My voice gave out completely and I lay there, mouth agape. I went through five minutes of agony in silence.

"If you're not well, I'm calling the doctor."

Through half-open eyelids I saw him put a hand on the phone. I didn't move. He lifted the receiver. He replaced it.

"But . . . what exactly's wrong with you?"

I refused to answer.

"Foster . . . Foster? I'm talking to you!" He came back beside me, and I felt his hand on my forehead. "Not really hot. A slight temperature perhaps. Foster—"

"Don't touch me. I forbid you to touch me."

"I'll make you some tea."

He disappeared from my field of vision. I stood up and went to the door without making a sound. I turned the knob only to discover that the door was locked and the key not there.

"You want to leave?"

Colin's voice made me jump.

"Open up right away."

"I thought you were at death's door!"

"Open up, I said!"

Sweat was running the length of my back, making me shiver. My legs refused to hold me up any longer.

"Go sit down again."

Colin took me by the arm and led me to the sofa where I collapsed.

"The tea will do you good, I'm sure."

He went back into the kitchen for a moment. My lips were trembling so violently that it seemed my energy was entirely concentrated on their quivering. My heart struggled to burst through the ribs. I recognized the first signs of fainting, just caught the sound Colin made as he put down his tray on the table. And then, very slowly, the light shrank to a pinpoint of infinity, like an implosion in my head.

The first sense to return was that of smell. Chinese tea, smoky aroma, I thought . . . The buzzing in my ears was too loud for me to hear the chink of a spoon against a cup, but my skin told me of the object's movement. I decided to open my lids. Colin was crouched in front of the table, stirring with a spoon.

"It's over?" he asked.

"Yes."

It was true, I did feel much better. I had sloughed off my anxiety and pain. Colin pushed the cup toward me. I grabbed it, spilling part of the tea on my fingers without feeling the heat. I drank down the burning liquid in one gulp, my tongue and palate too numb to react to this abuse. I avoided Colin's eye. I was ashamed, though relieved. What annoyed me most about Colin, basically, was that he was always right. He poured more tea. My watch read one-thirty.

"Hungry?" he asked calmly.

"No."

I owed him an apology but couldn't bring myself to make it.

"Would you like some cookies?"

"No."

"To dunk in the tea?"

I shrugged. How could he talk to me about eating? Involuntarily I raised my head. Colin was looking at me. I tried to escape his enormous eyes, surprised to see my reflection in them. Then tears ran down my cheeks, and for the second time that day I wept. There was neither hatred nor pity in the mirror of those eyes, only gentleness and understanding. He came to sit beside me and rested his hand on mine.

"You're ice-cold, Foster. The best thing would be for you to go home and rest. Get some sleep if you can."

We were still looking at one another, and I cried all the harder. Then I closed my eyes. I hated Colin seeing me this way. I was sure he was waiting for me to beg his pardon. But I wouldn't do it. Never. The warmth of his palm and fingers was finally transmitted to my skin. That exasperated me. Pushing him away, I bumped into the table as I got to my feet. The cups and saucers rattled.

"You think, maybe, that just because I'm sick, I'll let you fool around with me?"

He shook his head sadly. A sob escaped me. Unsteady on my feet, I reached the door and leaned against the frame.

"Open up."

Colin drew the keys out of his trousers pocket and unlocked the door, after which he turned his back on me and returned to finish his tea. In the hallway I pulled myself together. I closed Colin's door myself and went down one flight. I had completely forgotten to mention Mrs. Bernhardt.

Staggering like a drunken sailor, I let myself into my apartment and immediately went to bed. I avoided looking in the mirror, fearing what I surely would have seen there.

I proceeded to drown in the warm tides of sleep.

Dimly aware of the phone ringing, I reached out an arm as though to stop the alarm clock. It was ridiculous, of course. I groaned and gave up trying to stop it. Slipping my arm under the covers again, I went back to sleep. Unfortunately bad dreams bedeviled me. For a second or for five hours, I didn't know, but insistently enough to leave red and black lines beneath my closed eyelids.

The tick-tock I heard was real enough, though, as I held a course between day and night. Tick-light, tock-darkness, day-night, tick-tock, wake-sleep.

Eventually I got up, horrified by the touch of the sweat-drenched sheets. It was seven-thirty. Dabbing my face with a damp washcloth to dispel the nightmares, I unintentionally caught sight of myself in the bathroom mirror.

Damp curls were clinging to the back of my neck and my forehead. I was exceptionally pale, and my lips had faded from their usual red to white. The only traces of color on the unrecognizable face were from recent scratches. One of them, I remembered, had been caused by Florence Fairchild's ring.

And then there were my gray eyes—now bulging, swamped in blood, sweat, and salt. The irises, a pair of strange flowers, looked almost blue. Seeing myself thus, an astonishing abstract painting, I thought of Grindling Conrad. I was surprised to have no news from James, then remembered the phone call that had half-aroused me during the afternoon.

Going to the living room, I called James at his home number. I got his wife, who kept me there chattering for a good five minutes before releasing me to James.

"So, what happened?" I asked.

"Look here, buddy, it wasn't easy! First I had one dry run because Conrad wasn't there. Then I went back early in the afternoon, and that time I did find him. Well, I tell you, buddy, it was really something!"

Thus far James had been relatively incoherent.

I deliberately cut him off. "Fine, but what did you say to him?"

"Look, friend, the thing is that he didn't leave me an opening."

"How do you mean?"

"I began by saying that I was with the *Art Review*. He came back with 'a bunch of idiots, pedants, and incompetent scribblers.' So I talk to him about the show, and he goes, 'Those cretins, they only mutter to themselves.' Look here, you get the drift?"

"Yes. Go on."

"So I persist, and I tell him the magazine would like to do something on him. Really, I explain it all to him, you know, a whole pile of articles, trying to put on a show in a spiffy gallery. But, look here, that was really the one word not to say! He hands me this tirade on art galleries. Brother! I couldn't get in a single word. He's impossible. And what's more, he's enormous! No kidding, I was in a pretty tight corner. Well, look, what're we going to do now?"

"Listen, none of that changes a thing. Make arrangements with Spenser to photograph some paintings. Then you do a critique on them. I do a little piece, too, and another longer one on the Contemporary Arts Day itself and particularly on Conrad, which I'll send to Macland with a few flourishes so he'll run it. After that we'll apply our wits to finding some guy savvy enough to lend us a joint where we can hang them. When we've gotten that far, we'll alert Grindling Conrad to what we've cooked up."

"Good. Look here, friend, could you ask the lovely Florence to take care of the publicity?"

"Why not? You've given me a good idea, James."

"You serious?"

"Yes, absolutely."

As always, after talking with James, I felt a bit better. With his gift for simplicity and spontaneity he could always calm me down. I sat at my desk before a virgin page, knowing for a fact that I couldn't write a word. Fatigue filtered into my spinal column, gradually creeping up my neck, all the way to my brain. I was adrift in stormy clouds and rainy thoughts, sinking further by the second under the weight of my melancholy. On the blank page I jotted down two words: reflection-reality. It must have been about eight o'clock when Colin knocked, and I instantly let him in.

"Feeling any better?" he asked

"No."

"Listen, we're headed for a restaurant to celebrate. Uh . . . well, for Bruce and Sharon. I guess you wouldn't want to come along? I told them you were very sick. It's no less than the truth, I'm afraid." There was a hint of irony in his smile. "But, if any time you're really not well, you should call 911."

"You don't give a shit?"

"Oh, come on, quit that. . . . It's a devoted nurse you want? I'm not cut out for the job."

"Oh, go screw yourself!"

He burst out laughing, which made me furious.

"With anyone you please!" I added.

He stood there without moving or speaking. Very likely he was hoping I would apologize.

Suddenly voices reached us from the floors above. I was tempted to dart back inside but decided instead to brave their stares. Appearing first, Virgil reacted with slight surprise on catching sight of me.

"Oh, Foster . . . well, you *do* look awful."

"Goodness," said Beatrice. "You poor guy. First time I've ever seen you like this."

Bruce Conway didn't say a word, and Sharon Dowd didn't even glance my way.

"Don't you feel well, Daddy?" Anita piped, jumping off the last step.

Once more Colin grinned at me. Conway and Sharon went on downstairs without a pause, drawing Virgil and Anita along with them. Beatrice hesitated, a friendly smile on her lips.

"Well, then, get a good rest. If you like, I'll stop by in the morning to see how you are."

Her kindness touched me deeply, and I responded faintly to her smile. "Thank you," was all I could manage to say.

She had to hurry to catch up with the others. Colin was still there.

Bruce's voice floated up to us. "Hey, you coming?"

I felt a surge of resentment. Here I was, cast off, abandoned, suffering. And Bruce was attempting to tear away Colin so as to punish me, I was sure of it. I tried to hold him back. If only I could keep him from going off with the others . . .

"Well, then, I'll be going—" he began.

"No!"

"What?"

"Wait . . ."

If I apologized, he would stay with me, that much was certain. But I couldn't.

"Why?" he asked, visibly interested.

"Colin, come on!"

Again Bruce was calling him. Something like a duel of influence had opened between the two of us.

"Wait . . ." I couldn't bring myself to say anything else.

"Okay, so long," he said impatiently.

As he turned his back on me I knew only too well what it would take for me to keep him there.

"Colin . . ." I said faintly.

He put his hand on the rail and started downstairs.

"Colin . . ."

My voice was almost inaudible, an all but imperceptible croak.

"Wait . . ."

But it was no use.

My lips shaped a word that no sound carried toward him.

He disappeared down the turn of the stairway.

I was quite furious that they had left me this way. All of it just to drink to Bruce and Sharon's health. Let 'em drown in it! Suddenly I felt very tired. I got back into bed and went right to sleep. Without fully waking I caught the sound of feet going up the stairs. I turned over and woke up. Thinking that perhaps it was those idiots returning, I listened for a moment.

But no. It was one o'clock in the morning. I sat up, my ears straining. There was a strange sound, at first a faint tapping with a hollow reverberation. It reminded me of a drawn bow, vibrating after its arrow has been launched into the blue. It was disturbing. In this part of the building there could be nobody but me, Mrs. Bernhardt, and Josh Hardy. I got out of bed. Standing in the living room, I could not see the customary strip of light under the door, coming from the hall. Somebody had definitely gone by and turned them off. After a brief pause I ventured into the darkness. Stretching my hands out in front of me, I went up to the railing and grabbed hold of it. Breathing slowly, gently, I allowed the heavy atmosphere to sweep over me. Then it occurred to me to wonder what on earth I was doing out there on the landing like an idiot.

Leaning out, I tried to see through the shadows. I craned upward, searching. I knew I wasn't alone. It was as though the darkness were falling onto my face, crushing me, choking me. If I wished to see, I had only to reach for the switch. Instead I stayed put, still scanning the upper reaches from where I stood, beginning to make out the slats of the railing. But there was something that bewildered me, a zone of shadow floating in space above my head. It suddenly came to me that this was just like the night before, this impression of seeing an object swinging in the void. Retreating, I stumbled across a loose floorboard. I touched the frame of my wide-open door and brushed against the light switch.

I felt a light draft against my skin, caught something like a glimmer. Then a metallic clink reached me from the ground floor. I started violently.

I flicked on the switch, but the bright light gave me no pleasure at all, since it was to show me what I didn't wish to see. I glanced down, to find the cause of this new sound. From the bottom of the stairwell came the glint of a key ring.

And then I looked.

I wanted to shriek but couldn't make a sound. I wanted to hide or disappear. My hand slid along the wall where I had taken refuge. I got down on all fours and started crawling backward, my mouth silenced, my eyes blinded. I found it impossible to shut my eyelids. Desperate, still backing up, I tried to cry out. My foot touched a jutting step. I leaped forward, panting, and climbed the stairs as fast as my intractable legs would allow.

Reaching the sixth floor, I flattened out against the wall. Then I threw myself to the ground and caught up the rope in both hands. Arms twisting between the balusters, rubbing painfully against the wood, I struggled to raise a weight that seemed enormous. I saw my veins swelling under the effort, my fingers turning white at the joints. Sweat covered my forehead, and I let go.

I could hear the snapping of vertebrae.

Telephone, I should call someone. Glued to the wall, I made my way down again, but between the sixth and fifth floors, I could not avoid the sight. At first my eyes followed the rope and the knot, then rested on the yellow eyes, open and staring, the twisted smile and then the body, black and contorted.

And there was the hand.

The palm turned slightly forward and the fingers that had let go of the keys.

Finally I reached my door to find it snapped shut.

I raced down the stairs, stumbled across the entry court, and dashed out onto the street. I stopped, frenzied, looking for someplace to take shelter. At the end of the block I caught sight of a small group of people. The first I recognized was the tall figure of Virgil Sparks. There they were at last! I took a gulp of fresh air and ran toward them.

"Hey, look, it's—" began Virgil.

I fell to my knees on the sidewalk.

"What's happened to you, Foster?" Colin asked anxiously.

I couldn't answer. Beatrice insisted that I had to be taken home.

"No!" I shouted.

I grabbed Beatrice's wrists and squeezed with all my might, struggling against panic and another attack.

"Come along, Foster," said Colin softly.

"No!"

Sharon had stepped forward, and freeing Beatrice, I tried to stop her. I touched her leg as I collapsed onto the pavement.

"Foster," Beatrice implored, "get up, for heaven's sake!"

Suddenly I leaned over the gutter and vomited.

"He's really sick," she said. "We've got to do something."

"I'll go call a doctor," Virgil decided.

As he strode off rapidly toward the building I leapt clumsily to my feet and caught up with him.

"No!" I said, shoving him against the drugstore window.

I was enraged at my incapacity to express myself, but the anger momentarily restored my powers of speech. "She's dead! Don't go in!"

"What?"

"Don't go in!"

Colin was shaking me by the shoulders. "What're you talking about?"

My head was spinning; I saw the black sky, the pavement, the dark windows. I was struggling to hold onto a consciousness that was threatening to slip away. Brushing Colin aside, I grasped Bruce Conway's arm and dragged him with me into the entryway.

"No!" I hollered as the others made to follow us. "Don't come in!"

They stopped, undecided. As Bruce went into the building with me I closed the door behind us.

"Foster, listen to me. . . ."

He seemed angry. Unable to explain, I could do no more than hang onto the railing and look up. A sudden doubt overtook me. Could the whole thing simply be a nightmare? I watched him intensely, waiting for him to confirm my insanity. He looked up, and I could see him turn pale. He stared at me with wide-open eyes, then finally reacted. When he went back outside, I heard him asking Beatrice for the keys to her apartment, which, fortunately, was on the second floor.

"But what's going on?" asked Sharon, visibly panic-stricken.

"Stay there, don't come in!" Bruce ordered, again closing the door behind him.

Bruce dashed upstairs two at a time and went into Beatrice's apartment, leaving the door wide-open.

I slid to the ground, went flat on the cold tiles, arms covering my head and forehead pressed to the floor. I was trying to seal myself off, to escape. Deafening whistles and buzzing filled my ears. I couldn't see a thing. I was successfully beginning to drift off, withdraw. If only I could build a wall around me, close myself in.

Sirens wailed, echoed. Rapid footsteps started up the first flight. I smiled knowingly to myself. But it was only on hearing an unfamiliar voice say, "Shit, man, it'll be some fuckin' job gettin' this one down!" that I was finally able to black out.

7. In which we see that life goes on

When I woke up to broad daylight, Beatrice was sitting beside my bed. To my dismay I realized that I was quite all right. I had hoped to be at death's door for at least three months, but nothing of the sort. Bad luck was dogging my footsteps.

"Hi," I said.

Beatrice instantly looked up and smiled at me.

"How d'you feel?"

"Just fine. Worst luck."

Her features were drawn, like the face of a rag doll.

"It's you who should get some rest now," I remarked.

"Oh, you know . . . I couldn't have slept in any event. Colin kept me company. He's in the kitchen. It's all so horrible," she added with a shudder.

I decided to get out of bed. Though my legs were a bit wobbly, I realized after a couple of steps that I could walk with no real trouble.

"D'you think that's a very good idea?" Beatrice asked.

"Sure . . . don't worry."

Leaving the bedroom, I found Colin rummaging around in the kitchen cupboards, his back to me.

"Tell me, Bea, if the sugar is in the container marked flour, do you suppose we'll find coffee in the one marked tea?"

"No, the coffee's in the coffee tin."

"Oh, it's you!" he said, turning around.

"So it seems. Here, let me do it. Knowing you as I do, I can be pretty sure you'll louse up something."

I set about filling my Italian drip pot under Colin's inquisitive stare. Eventually he must have concluded that I looked

93

more or less normal. "Well, good," he declared. "I'll go warn Bea that breakfast is on the way to being ready."

With a steady hand I set up the tray, and when the boiling water spat in the flame, I was able to turn the pot the other way with no trouble whatsoever. I carried in the fixings and the toast, then the full cups. Beatrice and Colin were waiting at the table without a word. I sat down and began to hand things around.

"Could you pass me the butter, Foster," asked Colin, the only utterance in ten minutes. Oddly, we were all three starved.

"Whew, that's better," Beatrice concluded, pushing away her empty plate.

"Yeah."

"There's something I want to say," I ventured.

"Ah?" Colin responded, crossing his arms.

"Yes, I . . . it wasn't my fault."

"Your fault? Where'd you ever get such an idea, Foster?" said Beatrice, disconcerted.

I searched Colin's face intently. Perhaps he would understand what I was going through. He sighed and began to clear the table. I didn't want my attempt at explanation to die right there.

"I tried to tell you yesterday," I went on. "And then . . ." I blushed, recalling what had transpired between us.

"Well, what I mean is . . . I don't know how to put it!" I blurted. "There's too much in my head and not enough words to say it."

Discouraged, I rested my forehead against my palm. Leaning my elbows on the table, I tried to sort out my ideas.

"Actually," I began again, "it's as though I always knew what was going to happen. And I did nothing to prevent it."

"That's the kind of thing one always feels afterward," noted Beatrice. "It means absolutely nothing, for heaven's sake."

"No, no! That's not true. How can I get you to understand? What I lived through yesterday—I'd already gone through the day before. What is that? A premonition? I've no idea. I was out on the landing and I felt a presence, though I was completely alone. D'you see? No, you don't."

For a moment I closed my eyes. When I opened them, Colin had sat down again, apparently ready to listen this time.

"When I let go of the rope, I could hear her vertebrae crack."

"What?" Colin stiffened with horror. "What're you saying?"

"I tried to get her up . . . but I couldn't do it. And when I let go, I heard—"

"Oh, stop it, stop it!" Beatrice cried out, hands over her ears.

"You know, I saw her death . . . before. Or rather, I saw her as if dead. She was fully alive when I passed her, but I saw her as dead. I can't explain it any better. I knew, and I didn't do a thing about it. . . . But it isn't really my fault, is it? Sometimes you're aware of something but you can't do anything about it. Isn't that true?"

"Of course, Foster."

Colin's gentle voice calmed me instantly.

I insisted they leave. They had tons to do, and I assured them I was fine.

It was a relief to be alone at last. For a moment or two I simply wandered around the room, touching the furniture. Absolutely certain that I was back in a normal world, I breathed in air that wouldn't harm me. I washed the dishes with relish. Oh, the salutary joy of simple acts! Almost gleefully I tossed the last dry spoon into the drawer. The clink as it hit the others reminded me of a similar sound. Puzzled, I tried to recall where and when and what . . . Then it all flooded back.

I snatched up my jacket and went out. It was a shock to find myself once more in the stairway, though everything was terribly normal. Slowly I went downstairs, hugging the wall. On reaching the ground floor, I searched the base of the stairwell and I found. I bent over to pick up Mrs. Bernhardt's keys. I rubbed the cold metal till it warmed up. Actually, I had no idea what I intended to do with the keys. This one must be for the front door. And this one . . . I took a close look at the small, finely worked gilt key. Yes, surely it must be to a strongbox. Hearing footsteps in the entryway, I hid the keys in my pocket. Then I went to the mailbox to take out whatever was there—nothing but junk mail, needless to say.

"You're back on your feet?" Virgil remarked as he came in.

"So you see . . ."

"Does that mean you're okay now?"

"Sure." I was getting bored with these inquiries about my health.

"Beatrice was at your place, wasn't she?"

"Yes, but she left."

"Oh, I see."

Suddenly I caught an odd expression on his face. "Something out of whack?"

"Well, yesterday at the restaurant . . . We had a really bad set-to."

"No kidding. So you spoiled Bruce's evening?"

"Hey, listen! It's no laughing matter."

"Depends on the point of view," I rejoined.

"It's as though she were happy to stay with you just to be rid of me. Not that she wasn't worried, naturally. But, see . . . I'm not amused by that sort of thing. She's avoiding me."

"Perhaps you're partly to blame?"

"Well, Foster, I'm sure that you, of all people, can understand me."

"As a matter of actual fact, my friend, not terribly well. Beatrice is a peach, and you adore her. So where's the problem?"

"I thought you were against marriage!"

"I never said that. But that isn't where you're at, is it?"

"That is where, precisely! She's sending me around the bend with it."

I sighed. "Okay, listen. Suppose we went up to your place to talk? I feel a bit cold here."

And suddenly there I was, a marriage counselor.

"You know, Bruce was down with the same thing," Virgil said as we walked upstairs.

"With what?"

"Well, with . . ." He glanced upward, and I instantly understood.

"Ah. Yes."

"It's ridiculous, but all day I've been wondering what they've done with it."

"I don't quite follow you."

"The body . . . what have they done with it?"

"Don't know. It must be at the morgue."

"And after that, what?"

I hesitated. "Well . . . the family will see to it?"

"You think she had a family?"

"I don't know."

"It bothers me. Suppose there's no one. Then what happens?"

"I guess the city . . . well, I mean there's got to be some public agency."

"It's really getting to me. It's ridiculous to be worrying about her now that she's dead. We should have worried before. But all the same, what if there's no one?" Virgil seemed truly concerned.

"Perhaps we could take on the expenses."

"You think so?"

"Oh, it's certainly possible. So long as we pay . . ."

"Well, then, I'm agreed to paying." That idea seemed to reassure him.

"Don't worry about it. I'll see what we can do."

"You really think that . . . that you can?"

"Sure I can. I'm still of sound mind, aren't I?"

"Yes, yes," he was quick to reply.

We went into his apartment. At my request Virgil shut the wide-open window.

"Okay, getting back to Beatrice . . . ."

"You already know the whole thing." Virgil lit up a cigarette impatiently. "There's nothing more to say."

"What it boils down to is that Beatrice wants to move in with you in the expectation of eventually marrying you. Is that it?"

"Eventually! That's condition number one, yes!"

"You don't want to?"

"I'm not insane!"

"Okay, let's think it over. There should be some painless solution to the problem. Before vacating an apartment, you have to give at least a month's notice. Why not give yourselves that much time to try it out together? If necessary, she could always move back into her apartment. What it'll take is a few concessions from each of you. *You* will have to accept the idea of communal life, and *she* will have to give up this idea of marriage, at least for a while."

"That last part did it! Because sooner or later the topic will be back on the front burner . . . and here I was, hoping you'd back me up."

"You love her, don't you?" I persisted.

"Sure, but take Bruce, for instance—"

"That's got nothing to do with the case. Believe me, Sharon is no Beatrice!"

"Oh, I have no doubts about that. Nobody is like Beatrice," he said with a grimace. "Twelve-fifteen," he added, looking at his watch. "She should be coming home for lunch."

"She left very late because of me. Perhaps she decided to work on through to catch up?"

"That would surprise me. In her office they do as they like."

"Fundamentally, my good friend, there are things to be said for marriage. Just think, in your case you'd have no further worries. Beatrice would bring you her salary every two weeks."

"Ah, so? This is intended as humor?"

"No, indeed, I'm entirely serious."

"You imagine that I would go ask her for money?"

"Hell, you do it already."

"You've got some nerve, Tuncurry!"

"You certainly asked her for some dough to pay your rent, didn't you?"

"Oh, but that's different."

"In what way, different?"

"Well . . ." He looked at me, and we both exploded with laughter.

"Okay, you're right after all." He stretched and yawned. "Stay for lunch?"

"Sure."

It would not be the first time the two of us had eaten out of cans lifted from well-stocked cupboards. We were taking inventory of his culinary treasures when Beatrice walked in.

"What're you two doing?"

"Just what exactly do you think we might be doing in a kitchen, can opener in hand? You have thirty seconds to give the right answer," I said.

"Um . . . fly casting?"

"Dreadfully sorry, dear contestant, but you've just lost. The correct answer was: transforming a nondescript hash into an elegant dish!"

"I had no idea you were a magician," noted Virgil, casting a critical eye at the pot I'd just filled.

"I'm not, but I have lots of imagination."

"Well, at any rate, you seem in fine form, the two of you," said Beatrice, turning away.

"See?" Virgil whispered in my ear. "She's giving me a bad time again. What's more, she must think that you're on my side and that we're plotting something together."

"Pay no attention. Just set the table as though nothing's up."

When I'd carried in the vegetables and the stuff out of the can—which I'm incapable of adequately describing—Beatrice was reading *The Wall Street Journal* with her feet propped up on the table. Sitting across from her, Virgil was having a hard time keeping a straight face.

"Is it ready?" she asked without lifting her eyes from the page.

"Yes, m'lady," I replied. "Might we ask the exchange rate of the Swiss franc?"

"Rising, as always."

"Neat! Then my funds are safe."

"It's scandalous to own Swiss francs!" protested Virgil.

Beatrice folded her newspaper carefully and, after removing her feet from the table, pulled the chair in closer.

"What is this concoction?"

"This, madam? Why braised venison in Master Huntsman's sauce, flambéed in cognac."

"No fooling?"

"Absolutely," I replied. "The only thing is that venison isn't in season, there was no more cognac, and the Master Huntsman was delayed, replaced by the Mistress Huntsman."

"I see."

"Anyway, this way it's healthier," I persisted.

"That's still to be seen!" rejoined Virgil, nonetheless serving himself to a generous helping.

Beatrice looked us over, first one and then the other, with a raised eyebrow. She was clearly waiting for us to declare open war. I passed her the platter ceremoniously.

"Mrs. Sparks . . ."

"Hey, wait a minute there . . ." Virgil remonstrated, blushing.

"What? Ah, yes; in fact, Mr. Sparks has something he wants to say to you."

"Who? Me?"

"Come, come, Virgil. Courage. I'm with you one hundred percent, my friend."

"Traitor!" he said, turning on me.

"I'm listening," said Beatrice steadily.

"Well, we might agree to some arrangement—"

"Ouch! Not an auspicious beginning!" she cut in.

"No, wait!" Virgil exclaimed. "Well, I mean, there's living together. We could give it a try. That much I concede, but please, gimme some fuckin' peace with the marriage business!"

"Good." Beatrice sighed with relief. Then she began to eat. "That's all?"

"That's all, folks!" I noted with a smile.

"You're an odd one, Foster Tuncurry," said Beatrice, looking at me not unkindly. "Crazy in the evening, sick in the morning, normal at noon. . . . What are you like in the afternoon?"

"All three at once. Or something different. Who knows?"

That afternoon, as a matter of fact, I wrestled with my articles on Grindling Conrad. Picking up my old idea about reflection as reality for the connecting thread, I found no trouble at all with the inspiration, to my great surprise. After some hesitation I called my editor-in-chief, Macland. The conversation lasted exactly two minutes, of which one was spent with the operator. "You're in luck, we've got space," was what I drew as an answer. But I wasn't about to complain.

After that, I felt a strong desire to leave the house. Deciding to take a breather, I dropped off the article at the newspaper and walked over to *The Art Review,* where I had a number of things to discuss. It was rather a nice day, and between the bleat of a horn and the rumble of a truck, you could actually hear the occasional cooing of pigeons. I passed several attractive young women, and I was happy to be out of doors—even in the polluted air, the never-ending streams of cars, and the piles of trash. I paused in front of several store windows and felt a surge of longing as I gazed at a display of safari clothing. Ah, the pith helmets of the Kilimanjaro explorers, Lake Victoria, and "Dr. Livingstone, I presume." I would have to take myself on a trip like that one of these days.

On reaching my destination, I was delighted by the comic-strip scene of frenzy: "You mean to say it's not ready? Listen, did you take care of the . . . How's it going with those photos?"

I sought out James Coventry. He was in his office with three of his colleagues whom I vaguely knew.

"Hey there, Tuncurry! Nice of you to come and see us," said one of them as he caught sight of me.

I gave him a gracious smile, struggling in vain for his name.

"Hi, buddy," said James. "You know, you don't look so hot."

"No, I've had a couple of little problems with my health. Nothing serious. Anyway, here's the stuff I've written on Conrad."

"Sensational! Why don't you pull up a chair? We're about to have a little confab. Uh, look here, I don't think you know Willie, our new photographer."

"Pleased to meet you."

Willie nodded an enthusiastic greeting. "I went to take shots of the paintings this morning," he made a point of telling me with what I'd call pride.

"Okay, then . . . look here, Foster, did you remember about Macland?" James wanted to know.

"That's done," I assured him. "It'll be in the next issue. They had some space to fill."

"Stroke of luck! Here, take a look at our layout."

I glanced at the worktable. "You were just starting on it, I gather?"

James nodded. "Yeah. We had a bit of a time convincing them to use it in this issue. But that much is settled. So what's the next step?"

"We look for a gallery, you said!" put in the guy whose name I couldn't remember.

"Well, yes," James agreed. "But who? How? Where? When?"

"Just a moment, just a moment," I said.

"What?"

"Let's get a few things straight. What I want to know, to begin with, is whether the *Review* has decided to go all out for Conrad. I mean, has your editorial committee taken a clear position?"

"Look here, buddy, I'm the editor-in-chief," James replied.

"And Randolph's father is the publisher," he added with a jab of the chin toward the young man in glasses who hadn't yet opened his mouth.

"That's good enough?" I asked, point-blank.

Randolph cleared his throat. "Yes, yes," he whispered, turning crimson.

"Okay. Second question: is the *Review* ready to shell out if necessary?"

"Shell out? But we're broke, my friend!"

"Well, in that case, the problem will be to find some gent who'll let us have his place for free. That won't be so easy."

"But we'll be giving him some knockout publicity," said James with an emphatic nod. "Got any ideas?"

"Let's shoot for the top. I'm for Schmidt."

"You're kidding?"

"No. What've we got to lose? You're right, we'll be giving him a huge plug, and that couldn't be anything but tempting."

"What if he doesn't like the paintings?"

"That's not the way old Schmidt thinks. He'll be asking himself whether it'll pay. And the answer is yes, since we'll mention him, and favorably for once. That's that. Now for another point—the method of persuasion. I'm for a circuitous approach. And for that, there's a splendid object by the name of Florence Fairchild."

"You can't be serious!" James roared with laughter and banged the table with the flat of his hand.

"Sure I am . . . I'm willing to risk it."

"Well, man, that takes some bravado. So we'll let you wing it on your own?"

"Yes. Providing you can find me some quiet little nook with a telephone, hereabouts."

"Okay. You can have Jerry's office if you like."

Jerry . . . so that was his name.

"Third on the right as you go out."

I got to my feet. In Jerry's office I called the Schmidt Gallery. A woman answered.

"Hello. I'm sorry to bother you, but I'm trying to contact Ms. Fairchild. Can you give me a number where she can be reached?"

"Would you tell me who's calling, please? And this is in reference to what?"

"I'm an art critic, and I need to talk to Mr. Schmidt's press representative, if you please. It's quite urgent."

"I only have her home number, and I don't know if I can give it out."

"I assure you that this is an emergency."

"Well, all right. It's 226-0631."

"Thank you ever so much. I'll see that you're sent some flowers."

"Splendid," she replied with a laugh. "That's to the attention of Melanie."

"I won't forget. Goodbye, Melanie."

"Bye-bye, whoever you are."

Being a man of my word, I made a mental note: flowers for Melanie. The toughest part was yet to come.

"Hello?"

"Hello, Ms. Fairchild?"

"Yes, who is this?"

"Foster Tuncurry."

"What?"

"Foster Tuncurry. Is there some way we could talk without having it turn to disaster?"

"What do you want?"

"First of all, to ask you a simple question. Did you see the Grindling Conrad exhibition at that Contemporary Arts Day?"

"No."

I sighed. "I thought you were interested in painting. . . ."

"Oh, don't be abusive. I heard about Conrad, and someone told me he wasn't worth the trouble. . . ."

"You heard about him . . . someone told you. . . ." Already she was making me bristle. "You had one flight of stairs to climb and you didn't even do it?"

"But—"

"No, listen to me." I stopped, trying to keep calm. "What I saw of Grindling Conrad was enough to tell me that he is the first truly creative artist I've been privileged to see in ten years. A pity you didn't take in the exhibit. But now I want to propose something. Go up to Columbia, at least go take a look at the paintings if they're still on the walls. And if after that you can tell me that in your considered opinion it is bad, I promise to move to Alaska. If, on the other hand, you share my view—and let's add, incidentally, the view of all the *Art Review* editors—

would you agree to persuading Schmidt to put on a show? Don't forget that there would be lots of free publicity for the Schmidt Gallery. That's no small matter. But, above all, it's a matter of conscience. So how about leaving off our quarrels and joining forces in a glorious campaign for art!''

"In the line of flaming oratory, you certainly don't stint."

"Flattery will get you everywhere. I'll give you my number, and you can call me when you've made up your mind. How's that?''

"Mr. Tuncurry, I'm too much a lady to tell you what you can do with your phone number. Goodbye!''

She hung up. I rapped the desk with my fist. What a bitch! Vain, proud, ignorant, stupid . . . I went back to James' office.

"So?" he asked.

"It's not going to be easy, but I'm not giving up. For the moment I need Grindling Conrad's address."

He handed me a file card. I entered the address in my date book and handed the card back.

"I'm off."

"You're going there? To his place?"

"Yup. I hope he's in."

"Good luck!" James growled. "I'm warning you, it'll be entertaining."

"We'll see." I was a bit dubious about the entertainment part of it.

As I passed a florist I paused to order some flowers for Melanie, to be delivered to the Schmidt Gallery the following morning. Then I hailed a cab. I was happy to sit down, suddenly feeling quite weak. But I was keeping busy in mind and body, thereby successfully keeping certain thoughts at bay.

Grindling Conrad lived near Columbia in a somewhat dilapidated building that opened off an alley. I didn't even have to ring, because the door suddenly opened on a colossus with red hair. He stared down at me from his full six-foot-three without a ray of welcome.

"Is it me you're after?" he said.

I drew myself up as tall as possible. "If your name is Grindling Conrad, it's you I'm after. Though the expression

appears most aggressive and little in keeping with my intentions."

"Great gods, another speechifier! So lay it on me—and fast.
I'm in a hurry."

"I believe you've already had dealings with James Coventry?"

"Don't know him."

"Yes, you do, *The Art Review.*"

"Oh, yes! Another one I put out the door."

I cleared my throat. "To state it quickly the magazine and I
have decided to do a piece on you. It's already in the works, in
fact. What I mean to say is that we've decided to do it whether
you approve or not."

"What?" His frown failed to scare me. I was even reassured.

"So as to conceal nothing, I should mention that I'm negoti-
ating with the Schmidt Gallery." I was getting a bit ahead of
myself.

"Oh, you are, are you?" This time his voice was frankly
menacing.

"And even if it doesn't work out with them, there are others.
I've taken up your cause."

"Really?"

"Yes, without commission, without personal gain. I even
stand ready to spend some of my own money if necessary. I'm
sick of dreaming that if I had lived in van Gogh's day I'd have
watched him croak along with the rest of them."

"Who are you, anyway?" he asked, leaning against the
doorjamb, a sign that he wasn't in that much of a hurry.

"My name is Foster Tuncurry, and I—"

"And you wrote *Malicious Delights* on Hieronymus
Bosch."

"So I did. You've read it?"

"Three times."

"Ah? Perhaps you'd like to read what I've written about
you?"

I held out copies of my two articles, certain that in any event
he would appreciate what I had to say about the Arts Day
panelists. With his left hand he respectfully grasped the articles, and I was surprised to observe a hand of such delicacy that
it didn't suit the wrestler's physique of its proprietor.

"Come on in."

He stood back to let me pass, and I entered his lair. Everything had been conceived and constructed for painting. And I had some difficulty locating a bed on which to sit down, there being no chair at all. Conrad had co-opted the only existing stool.

"So it appears you are acting without my say-so?"

"You would have said no. We sidestepped."

"I loathe art galleries."

"Me too. But it's the necessary step before the Whitney or the Modern."

"I have no use for museums, either."

"We have to be realistic." I shrugged. "There's no other way."

"You seem pretty blasé."

"Oh, far worse. I'm cynical. But I know how to fight when necessary."

"I'm worth your while?"

"I'm beholden to you for arousing my emotions. That's more than I've been able to say for a long time about painting."

He smiled at me.

"I might just persuade myself that you're likable."

"I don't ask that much," I said.

"And you sincerely believe that stuffed goose of a Schmidt will take me on? *Me?*"

"I'm counting on it. It won't be easy, that's for sure, but I wouldn't rule it out."

"How about a drink? I have some real Irish whiskey. It would put a bit of color in your cheeks. Are you always so pale?"

"I'm not very well at the moment."

"And even in that state, you're going to this trouble for me? It's very flattering."

"Action staves off depression."

"It's that bad? Well, then, a whiskey?"

"I'd prefer a cup of tea."

"Tea?" He was incredulous. "Sorry, but I simply don't keep any around."

"Well, then, nothing, thanks." Noticing a rapid drop in my approval quotient, I quickly amended myself. "Well, okay, but really just a taste."

"That's more like it!" He got to his feet, rubbing his hands together. "You'll see, it packs a wallop!"

I kept my mouth shut while he cheerfully poured me half a glass of whiskey and a whole one for himself. I watched him swallow great gulps, and after some hesitation, I wet my lips.

"So?" he asked. "Fantastic, right?"

"Why, yes, excellent." And that was the truth. "You're Irish?"

"Celtic, dear sir, Celtic!" he exclaimed.

"Celtic . . . from Ireland?"

"No, absolutely not. I'm Danish on my mother's side, hence Viking, and Scottish on my father's side, hence Celtic."

"A Pict?" I asked with some amusement.

"Oh . . . there's nothing to say I'm not, I suppose."

"Grindling Conrad, that's your real name?"

"Surprising as that may seem, yes. I've often thought of adopting a pseudonym on the order of John Smith or Alfred Jones. As for you, you have a rather original name."

"Yes. But my ancestors were convicts. I come via Australia. It's not so glorious, but I like the idea that my great-grandparents were either in fetters or denizens of a London brothel. Those people made America too. Sometimes I wonder how we have the nerve to talk about our great American nation and all those good and true Americans . . . entirely based on the outcasts of European society—criminals, prostitutes, Puritans, and a few intellectuals in exile to keep them in order."

"It's apparent that you have a rather iconoclastic turn of mind."

After a sip of my drink I remarked, "You ought to have some Scotch."

"I'm out of touch with Scotland now. In fact, my mother married an Irish farmer the second time around."

"Your father died?"

"No." The artist submitted willingly enough to my interrogation. "He married a Canadian woman and is living in New Zealand."

"And why not?"

"Right. But we've drifted a good way from our topic."

"All I'd like is to be given a free hand."

"And to do whatever you see fit with it?"

"Exactly. First off, I'd like to see more of your work."

"There it is." He made a circular sweep of the hand.

Placing my glass on the floor, I stood up. I was immediately drawn to a canvas in the background. I read "Homage to Brueghel" and recognized a modern version of *The Fall of Icarus*.

"I'm sure you like that one," he said with a smile.

"Impossible to hide anything from you. And this one, it's . . . *The Sunken City*."

I gazed in turn at other paintings with provocative titles, then came to a halt, quite perplexed, in front of the last: *After Renoir*. And it was actually possible to see Renoir in it but as though analyzed, thought out anew, recreated.

"You like Renoir?" I asked, astonished.

"Yes, of course. Why?"

"Because . . . I don't know, it somehow doesn't fit in with you."

"What a strange idea."

I stood there in silent disapproval.

"There's such emotion in Renoir," he went on. "And perfect motion, a gentleness. You feel suffused with joy from seeing the bows in the little girls' hair."

"Well, perhaps so. But it leaves me cold." As I pronounced those words, I felt a chill in my bones.

"Are you feeling all right?"

"I'm a bit tired. Not very clever of me."

"You should get some rest."

"I shall. And you'll let me follow my own lead?"

"It appears I have no choice!"

"Fine. I'll give you my number in case you want to reach me. I'll keep you posted."

As I leaned over to pick up the glass I could feel a throbbing in my temples and decided to forgo the rest of the drink.

I'd been dozing for some twenty minutes when my telephone rang. Though I had no desire to stir, I dragged myself into the living room, swearing I'd buy an answering machine so as to be free of the bloody contraption.

"Hello," I growled.

"Mr. Tuncurry?"

The grave tone of the voice made it instantly identifiable.

"Florence? Ms. Fairchild?" I immediately corrected myself.

"Yes. Foster . . . there's something I have to tell you."

"I'm all ears."

"It's simply that I do think for myself and do have my own opinions."

"Oh?"

"And, though I have not the least desire to ingratiate myself with you, I have to admit—purely out of a love for art, of course—that your Mr. Conrad captivates me. His work, at least. And alas, I therefore won't have the pleasure of knowing that you've left for Alaska."

"You fill me with joy," I replied emphatically. "What do you intend to do next?"

"Well, I suppose this is the ideal time to inaugurate the basement room we've just completed underneath the gallery. That would allow us to move right ahead on it, without having to change the least detail in our schedule. It would hardly be politic to cancel our other commitments."

"As for me, I'd be delighted to hear they'd been entirely eliminated." I couldn't resist a bit of banter. "But I'll settle happily for the basement. As for free publicity you won't have to lift a finger. It's already launched. Unfortunately, it may even be a bit early."

"Would it be possible to add an insert in *The Art Review* announcing the show?"

"No problem, I'll take care of it. But what about dates?"

"How about a week from Monday?"

"Really? But does Schmidt know about all this?"

"I wouldn't be charging ahead this way if he didn't. I've made arrangements with a responsible firm to move the canvases from Columbia directly to our place. But there's still room for more of them."

"I'll see to it."

"No need, that's already done too," she replied.

"What did he say?"

"Who?"

"Grindling Conrad."

"Nothing. He didn't even look surprised."

"No, that figures. I gave him to understand that I was taking his interests in hand."

"That's what I thought. Aside from that, the girls at the gallery spent the end of the day filling out the invitations, addressing envelopes, and licking stamps. They're on their way. I mailed them myself. You see, publicists sometimes do their work properly."

I bit my lip, deciding to laugh.

"Mr. Tuncurry, the problem is that there are often imperatives and impediments of which you would not have the vaguest idea. I'll trust you to do the announcements in the *Review*. At no charge, of course."

"At no charge, I promise."

"Good. I suppose I'll have the occasion to meet you again in the very near future, worst luck?"

"Ah, yes, worst luck. I'm afraid so."

"In that case, see you soon . . . Foster."

"So long lovely friend . . . of the arts."

Before she hung up, I caught the hint of a laugh. I rang up James to tell him of my exploits, which he received with many a "look here" and "buddy." He wholeheartedly accepted the burden of doing some publicity in order, so he said, to make his modest contribution. As I put down the receiver I looked with some satisfaction and admiration upon that marvelous instrument, the telephone.

I settled into my work chair and breathed deeply for a moment or two. It was seven-fifteen when Beatrice stopped by to see how I was doing.

"So, feeling better?" she said with a smile.

Sitting down on the sofa, she gazed at the rents caused by Agamemnon.

"I don't know what you did to Virgil," she went on, "but I've never seen him so charming."

"I don't think I did much to him at all."

"By contrast, Bruce has never been so disagreeable."

"The bad influence of Sharon and her adorable daughter, no doubt."

"No, that's not at all what I meant. I'm surprised that he makes so light of your health. What exactly went on between the two of you?"

"Apparently we don't see things eye to eye. I detest that woman, and I said so quite openly. If you ask me, he's making the mistake of his life."

"I'm sure you're wrong. But that doesn't explain his attitude. When I ran into him just a while ago, I quite naturally mentioned you. And you know, he turned on his heels without a word. It made me feel odd, I swear. It's as though he's bearing me a grudge too."

"Let's hope he gets over it. When that bitch drops him, he'll come back to us."

"You shouldn't talk that way, Foster. It's not surprising he doesn't take it kindly. Sharon isn't what you think she is. I feel you're on the wrong track. Bruce lacks self-confidence, and that makes him nervous and irascible. Furthermore—"

"Listen, I'm fed to the gills with Bruce Conway! So please do shut up about him!"

"Okay, okay. . . ."

I was waiting for her to leave. She realized it and stood up. "So, I'll be off to find my fond quasi-husband. You ought to go by and see Colin."

"Why?"

"Because he's very worried about you."

Her tone of voice made it all but an interrogation.

"I'm not about to spend my time passing out bulletins on my health to the whole building."

"He's been wondering what you had. Me, too, as a matter of fact."

"An attack of tetany. I had it all through my childhood. It isn't serious. Anyway, it's over."

"Maybe. All the same, you don't look your best."

"No. With that whole business . . ."

We exchanged uneasy glances.

"At any rate, it didn't help my nerves."

"I can well imagine. Well, now . . . good night. Sleep well."

"Thanks. Bye."

I watched her disappear around the turn of the stairs. She went down one flight, hence to her own apartment. Perhaps Virgil wasn't in yet. Putting on my jacket, I, too, went out. I had decided to go up and see Bruce Conway. On the way by Colin's door, I debated about ringing his bell. But I kept on going. There were people at Bruce's, but I knew only too well who they were, and decided against going in.

Thrusting my cold hands deep into my pockets, I felt Mrs. Bernhardt's key ring. On impulse I climbed to the top of the stairs. I wondered if Josh Hardy had heard the news. In any case, I had no intention of talking with him about anything.

I opened the door to Mrs. Bernhardt's apartment. I found the light switch on the right and flicked it on, carefully closing the door behind me. The furniture was simple but out of style, the carpet terribly worn. On the central wooden table were two yellowing lace doilies and a singularly ugly vase. Beside the kitchen door stood the imposing bulk of a sideboard with a display of decorated plates.

I found myself smiling as I faced a bureau-top bearing black-and-white photographs in frames draped with black ribbon, and a seven-branched candlestick. I looked at the figures in the snapshots. There were only two of them, but they had been taken at different periods. Her husband, I surmised, and her son. Her son as a baby, as a boy of five, of twelve. . . . And a last in which he stood very straight and tall but awkward in his uniform.

I glanced at the Formica kitchen. There was a calendar with pictures of dogs and cats. Several posters and some double-page spreads out of magazines had been tacked to the wall. Only views of Israel, nothing but Israel. One showed a cemetery of white tombstones with Jerusalem in the background. Next I turned to the bedroom where, against the dingy, flowered wallpaper hung a large photograph of the Wailing Wall, surely taken on a Friday evening. On the bedside table I found a medal with an inscription on the back: "Samuel Bernhardt, died honorably in Vietnam, March 23, 1967." I sighed. Poor woman. She apparently had but one child, and he died in the war. Mrs. Bernhardt had been living in Stairway C for a long time, at least fifteen years. According to the building superintendent, her husband had died from an accident suffered on a public works project. That had happened a good sixteen years ago.

I looked into the bathroom where the basin was cracked, the bathtub in disrepair, and the toilet steadily trickling. A new coat of paint was badly needed, and in places the plaster had cracked and scaled away. I sighed again.

Back in the living room, I opened the doors of the sideboard. It was practically empty aside from a few pieces of chipped china and a bottle of orange liqueur. I poured some into a small glass, then set about searching for the strongbox to go with the little gilt key. I found it in the top cabinet drawer. Out of curiosity I also glanced into the other drawers. There wasn't much—some candles, some matches, and a book in phonetic Hebrew.

Setting my glass down beside the little box, I drew up a chair. I took a sip and made up my mind to insert the key in the shaky lock. Turning it twice, I raised the lid. On top rested a letter of dismissal bearing her name, dated June twenty-third of this year. Next, a passport belonging to her husband, Jacob; Samuel's military papers; and a photograph. It was of a young black woman holding in her arms a little black girl dressed all in white, with braids and bows like butterflies. She must have been two or three years old. On the back of the print was written "September '42, Chicago." Then I found a newspaper clipping: "This morning a four-year-old girl, Rachel Bernhardt, was struck by a school bus. She died at the Central Hospital without regaining consciousness." How could she have cut out and kept that clipping, that horror of impersonality and indifference? On the bottom of the coffer there was a child's link bracelet inscribed with the name of Rachel and appended with a few charms of poor quality—a twisted horseshoe, a small bell that still tinkled, a star of David, and a nondescript animal that might be a doe.

Studying the photograph once more, I realized something that would never have occurred to me before. Mrs. Bernhardt had once been young, happy, and pretty. At least until September 1942. There was nothing more in the chest but a small pink box. It contained a tarnished wedding ring and a baby tooth. On the inside of the ring, simply a date: "17 March '38." Trying it on my ring finger, I found it too small. It must have been hers. Keeping out the snapshot and the bracelet, I replaced the other objects. I closed the lid, locked it, and returned the strongbox to the cabinet drawer.

I finished the drink, then washed the glass, dried it, and put it back on the kitchen shelf along with the bottle. Returning to the table, I gazed once more at the faces of the mother and daughter. How beautiful that child had been! I ran the bracelet between my fingers, over and over. The little bell kept on tinkling.

With my arms on the table I rested my forehead on my right hand, which still held the bracelet. And I began to cry. Losing all notion of time, I sobbed for a long, long while. Eventually feeling a cramp in one shoulder, I straightened up. I automatically looked at my watch. It was nine-twenty. Touching my cheeks with a numb hand, I realized that I had been crying without tears for some time. I slipped the snapshot into my wallet and the bracelet into my pocket, then stood up, taking a last look around the room. I opened the door, switched off the light, and went out onto the landing. Feeling my way along the wall, I started downstairs.

I passed Bruce's door without pausing, then Colin's. On my own doormat I found the cat. I could see his eyes glowing in the dim light and felt the rub of his tail against my legs. He even purred, which exasperated me. I tried to brush him away but gave up.

"Wretched animal," I hissed.

Upstairs a door swung open, casting a bright beam of light across the stairwell.

"Foster? Is that you?"

Colin was calling me. I didn't move, waiting there without answering.

"Foster?" he repeated.

Then he went back inside. I wondered how he could have heard me. I was about to reenter the warmth of my apartment when an idea suddenly came to me. I went back up to the sixth floor, still careful not to make a sound.

Going straight to Mrs. Bernhardt's kitchen, I took down the picture of the cemetery overlooking Jerusalem, scanning it for some clue, a map, a place name. But there was no precise indication of the cemetery's location. I folded the picture, undoubtedly clipped from some magazine, and put it in my pocket.

I had just made a promise to Rachel.

8. *"How bitter is my fate . . ."*

—*On the Lagoons,* poem by Théophile Gautier set to music by Hector Berlioz.

Early that morning several ideas were chasing one another inside my head. I tried to sort them out. To begin with, I wrote Vanessa Poretski and invited her to the Grindling Conrad exhibition. Next I wheedled Florence Fairchild's address out of a young woman at the gallery, following which I went to the post office and then to the neighborhood florist, where I ordered some red roses to be sent to Ms. Fairchild.

Then it required all the courage at my command to enter the local precinct house. Resting my elbows on the counter, I waited patiently for a cop to take notice of me.

"What's your business?" asked the one across from me without looking up.

"I'm here about the death of Mrs. Bernhardt, which occurred during the night of the seventeenth to the eighteenth of this month. I'd like to know where the body is now and what the procedure is for taking charge of the funeral arrangements."

He looked at me with a frown. "You're a member of the family?"

"No, that's just it. But she has no family, and that's why I—"

"Just a moment, please."

He stood up to open a file drawer behind him.

"Bernhardt . . . how do you spell that? Oh, wait, I've found it. Suicide by hanging, 26 Sullivan Street, Stairway C. What's your name?"

"Tuncurry. I live in the same building. Some of the tenants want to pay for a proper funeral. You see?"

"Very good, but it's probably too late."

"Already?"

"I think so. You should go to the mortuary. I'll give you the address and an authorization." He filled out a small form.

"Is there some way to call in to alert them?"

"I'll do that. Just a moment." He held out a pink card and pen. "Write your name here."

Then I listened as he dialed. "Hello? Give me Room 6B, please. Max? It's Harry at the Precinct. Mornin'. Listen, did you get the remains of a Mrs. Bernhardt on the night of the seventeenth? . . . Yeah, that's right, a suicide. . . . She's been claimed? No? Right, no family? Okay, I'm sending you someone who's taking over. . . . What? Sent to the crematorium? Maybe it hasn't been done yet? Yeah, please. . . . Yup, thanks. . . . I'd very much appreciate that, Max. . . . So long."

"So?"

"He's going to try to stall," he replied with a smile.

"But they can't just go and cremate her, can they? She was Jewish. She needs a proper Jewish funeral. That's the least we can do!"

"What can I say? Go to Room 6B and ask for Max. That's all I can suggest."

With a sigh I thanked the officer for being so helpful. And, in fact, this was the first time I had met the likes of him.

I flagged a cab and steamed over to the morgue, which turned out to be part of the immense Bellevue Hospital complex. At the door I asked for directions from a man in a gray uniform. For a good ten minutes I wandered about in endless corridors, finally managing to unearth Max, who was puffing away right under a NO SMOKING sign.

"I been waiting for you. Let's have the card," Max said.

I drew the pink slip out of my pocket.

"I'm real sorry," he said, obviously not giving a damn.

"Sorry? Why?"

"It's too late. All I can do is give you a pass for the crematorium. You can take it from there with them."

"But has it been done or not?"

"It's down in the book for today, but mebbe it hasn't been
done yet."

"Where do I go?"

"As you leave this door just follow the signs." He handed
me a green card.

I dashed out and, taking my bearings from the signs, ran
along at top speed. Then I found myself in another part of the
huge, oppressive structure. I went in and was immediately accosted.

"Hey, you! Where're you going?"

"I'm trying to take possession of a body before it's turned to
ashes." I showed him the pass.

"Oh. Yeah. Unfortunately that's usually done every day by
dawn. . . . Follow me."

He led me down meandering hallways lined with heavy
slabs. Behind each one of them was a body. I shuddered.

"Stay here," the man ordered.

He vanished through a narrow door, abandoning me in this
sinister labyrinth. Digging my hands deep into my pockets, I
took in my surroundings anxiously. All of a sudden I was fully
aware of the grotesque situation into which I had thrust myself.
Here I was, tracking down a cadaver, and just exactly what for?
I wondered.

The man in the gray uniform reappeared. "Sorry . . . like I
said, they finish up here very early. I'm very sorry."

I took a step or two without the least idea of how to find my
way out. As I started off slowly, feeling terribly guilty, I heard
the door open again.

"Hey, you! Sir!"

I turned back with a new gleam of hope.

"Sir, are you the one who came for the, uh, Bernhardt remains?"

"Yes, I'm the one."

In his gray shirt and trousers he looked strangely like his co-
hort. "Would you sign here?"

He indicated a line at the bottom of a lengthy form. I signed.

"And there, would you please print your name and address."

I complied, but without any idea of what it was for.

"Thank you. Please wait right here. I'll be back."

Without reacting, I watched his retreating form. When he returned, he was carrying a funerary urn, which he handed me. "There you are," he said in a tone of complete satisfaction, and disappeared once more through the door.

I stood there speechless, then began to laugh. To laugh! I couldn't stop. My laughter echoed among the black slabs, amplified as it ricocheted off the ceiling. I laughed till my sides ached. And I didn't even know what I had signed.

I carried the horrible object home. Placing it on my table, I mulled the matter over. The best solution would probably be to get in touch with a rabbi, who would say a few prayers and find a place for her in a Jewish cemetery. But that was not what I had in mind. I actually intended to follow my sacred principle, which goes, "Why do something simply when you can make it complicated?"

Making a quick foray to the bookstore on Spring Street, I returned with a guidebook. Then, spreading out the picture I had taken from Mrs. Bernhardt's kitchen, I opened to the page called "Jerusalem and Environs" and began to read. Thanks to the location of the Dome of the Rock in the photograph, I had a pretty clear idea of the orientation. Eventually I found a few lines that seemed to relate to the site pictured.

". . . A narrow road that runs between peaceful flower gardens, olive groves, and stands of pine trees, above Gethsemane, then through the melancholic Jewish cemeteries above the Valley of Cedron. . . ."

It was a minor victory. After marking the page, I closed the book.

Feeling that I couldn't leave the urn exposed to all eyes, I put it away in the bottom of my closet. Then I reflected that Mrs. Bernhardt was entitled to at least one brief prayer. But I only knew the Lord's Prayer and the Hail Mary. I settled for the Lord's Prayer, which was, ultimately, as much hers as mine.

I placed the little bracelet and the two photographs beside the guidebook, gazing at them in turn as I gradually formulated a plan.

"All right," I said, my mind made up.

I rapidly looked up an address and phone number. First of all, get the information. I phoned the Israel Consulate General.

"I would like to know when it would be convenient for me to come by and settle a delicate matter."

"Of what nature, sir?" said a tired voice.

"Uh . . . a repatriation."

"The office is open from ten to one-thirty, Monday through Thursday. Ask for the emigration department."

"Thank you. Goodbye."

Another outfit that wasn't overextending itself—three and a half hours, four days a week! Since I had gotten up very early, it was still only eleven-forty, and I wouldn't have far to go. I'd give it a try.

Twenty minutes later I was there. I had to pass a security check, show the passport I'd fortunately brought for identification, and answer several questions before I was allowed to enter. I was handed a number and told to sit down and wait. At that point I understood why the office was open such a short time: There were enough people in the waiting room to last six hours. At two forty-five I was admitted to a room packed almost to capacity and directed to a man at the far end near the window. Though I went and stood in front of him, he took no notice of me but kept on scribbling, his glasses balanced on the tip of his nose.

"That's that," he finally said with evident satisfaction. He pushed aside a pile of files and leaned back, his elbows resting on the arms of his chair.

"What may I do for you?"

I cleared my throat, sensing that it wouldn't be easy going. "Well, this is a slightly, um . . . special case."

"Oh, just like all of them."

"To be brief, I would like to take the remains of a deceased woman to Israel."

"Ah, I see. Does this person have family there?"

"No."

"What city did she come from?"

"I haven't the slightest idea."

"But how . . . ?"

"I'm not a member of her family."

"Oh. But she is Jewish?"

"Yes, yes. No problem there."

The official persisted. "Fine, but . . . she is an Israeli, is she?"

"Beg your pardon?"

"She is a citizen?"

"Uh, no."

"But, you see . . ." He pondered for a moment. "As you say, this is a special case. Please wait here. I will be right back."

I waited patiently a while longer. After all, I had been doing it all day long. When he beckoned to me from across the room, I went over. He led me to a quieter section of the consulate where I found myself face-to-face with an extremely severe-looking man.

"Sir," he said by way of salutation.

On impulse I responded with a nod.

"Would you kindly give a concise account of your problem?"

This time I was frankly up against it. "Well, it's quite simple," I began. "A Jewish woman in my building just died, and I would like for her to be buried in her own country."

"But I understood that she was an American."

"So she was, in fact, but not at heart."

"Do you have any notion of the problems involved?"

"Absolutely, but I will take care of everything. All I need is authorization to carry the ashes of this woman who was, uh . . . very pious."

"The what?"

"Beg your pardon?" I was stalling for time.

"What did you say? The ashes?"

"Well, actually, yes. You see, they won't take up much space."

"Are you making light of all this, sir?"

"Not in the least! I . . . it's the city, it's their fault!" I scratched my head, groping for words. "She had no family. She was cremated by mistake. I obtained permission to claim the urn, and I would like this unfortunate person to have at least the burial she would have wanted. In hallowed ground. Besides, I must add that it is in response to a wish she expressed in my presence."

"There's no will?"

"Unfortunately no. It was a last oral request."

"Sorry, there's nothing to be done."

"But all I'm asking is an entry permit. I'll take care of the rest."

"It is impossible, sir. There is no family, no will, and no rights of citizenship. We accept immigration for the living, not the dead."

"I see," I said bitterly. "Dead, they're no use to you."

"Where would it get us if we began to honor this sort of request?"

"To heaven, perhaps."

He shrugged and closed the interview as he had begun. "Sir."

"You may just see me again." I sighed and stood up. "I won't give up so easily. Or rather, I'll set my sights higher. There must be a way to reach the consul or the ambassador."

Shuffling through a welter of papers, he didn't look up.

"Idiot," I hissed as I left.

But calling him names wasn't going to fix anything. The moment Mrs. Bernhardt was involved, everything seemed to go wrong one way or another.

I passed Bruce Conway on the stairs. The moment he caught sight of me, he turned away.

"Hi," I said.

He kept on without answering.

"You're off work mighty early," I continued. I was about to open my mouth again when I saw Colin bounding upstairs. Bruce and he greeted one another cheerfully.

"Hey, so there you are, Foster."

As Bruce disappeared out the door Colin scowled. "What have you gone and said to him this time?"

"Me? Nothing at all! I said hello, and he coldly ignored me. He's the one who's angry, not me."

I brushed him aside as I went for my door. He stayed put, hands in his pockets, waiting for me to invite him in, which I had no intention of doing. Reacting to the situation with remarkable speed, he stepped forward, placing his body halfway through the doorway as I was trying to close up.

"Mr. Shepherd, I would like to remind you that you live upstairs."

"Yes, I know."

And this time he stepped all the way into my living room.

"Colin, I don't feel like talking to you."

"You never feel like doing anything."

I sighed, and suddenly it came to me that never before had I sighed so often. I sat down, resigned. "What do you want?"

"Who, me?" He assumed a look of wide-eyed surprise. "I'm not after anything." He sat down at my table and gazed at the things I had left there. "What is all of this?" He picked up the little bracelet, then the photographs.

"Don't touch them!" I made a dive for him and snatched the things from his hands. He watched me, astounded, while I put the things away in the bureau drawer.

"Foster, is something wrong?"

"What gave you the clue?"

"Why are you behaving like this?"

I couldn't bring myself to explain it to him. I was thinking of Rachel. ("A garden inclosed is my sister, my spouse; a spring shut up, a fountain sealed." The verse from *The Song of Solomon* was running through my head.)

"What?"

I didn't answer.

"There's really something not quite right in your head, my poor friend."

"Don't give me that pitying tone! It's exasperating. And what's more, everything is just fine in my head, my poor Colin!"

Sensing that I was on the verge of saying ugly things to him again, I tried to keep still. But he didn't want to let it go.

"Foster," he began, "I can easily understand that you've been shook up by what's happened, but it's time to get hold of yourself and—"

"Cut it out! I'm sick of your sermons. Get out, hear me? Get lost!"

I grabbed hold of him and dragged him to the door, shoving him out so violently that he crashed into the stairs.

"Ouch!" he cried out, falling to his knees.

Seeing that his eyes were brimming with tears, I hurried to close the door.

"Foster!"

His plaintive call was more than I could bear. When I went back out, he was holding his left knee, sobbing with pain.

"You hurt me!" His tone of voice and attitude were those of a child who's been roughed up at recess. Without raising his head he glanced up at me accusingly, as though sulking.

"I'll be lucky if my kneecap isn't dislocated."

Pulling his hands away, I raised the pant leg. His leg was bleeding slightly. I pressed my handkerchief to the cut and stood up. "I'll get some disinfectant."

"What's going on?" Suddenly hearing Bruce's voice right behind me, I jumped.

"He's banged into the stairs," I said.

"Banged into the stairs, sure! You pushed me!"

Bruce jabbed his chin in my direction. "Wasting your time, Shep, with this jerk."

I lashed out at him, and he struck right back.

"Stop!" Colin cried.

"You can't say I started it!" I retorted.

Bruce Conway had his clenched fists raised, clearly ready to fight.

"Bruce, stop it." Colin stretched out a hand to touch him. "Leave him alone. He's not himself."

"He never has been!"

"It's the two of you that're going mad, for chrissake." I turned my back on them and went off for some peroxide and gauze pads. I came back with my first-aid kit, determined not to get angry. Bruce had sat down on the steps beside Colin and was examining the injured knee.

"Nothing's broken," he remarked after probing the joint. "You do seem mighty sensitive."

Colin pouted in disapproval. "But it hurts."

"You're putting me on. It's nothing but a scratch!"

"Ow!"

Bruce couldn't help laughing at Colin's expression while I disinfected the cut.

"Courage!" he exhorted.

I applied myself to doing him up in a bandage three times too large, still trying to keep a straight face.

"You think that'll do?" Bruce asked in an anxious tone. "A splint might help. Think you can walk without a crutch, Shep?"

"Don't call me Shep or Col, please," replied Colin, out of sorts.

"There, that's done," I said.

Colin bent over to admire it.

"Some fine bandage for baby, that is," Bruce said pointedly, delighted at the chance to watch Colin fly off the handle.

"Perhaps it is a bit much," mumbled the patient with a dubious tilt of the head.

"Whaddya mean! It's hardly enough. Perhaps you'll need to be carried upstairs?" Bruce kept at him.

Colin reached out a hand. "Help me get up."

"Come off it!" hooted Bruce.

I took Colin's hand and pulled him toward me. His grip tightened once he was on his feet. He kept my hand captive, showing no sign of releasing it. When I discreetly attempted to disengage it, he only squeezed harder.

"All right," he pronounced gravely.

Noticing how I was being held, Bruce Conway raised an eyebrow. Then our eyes met, each of us actually as surprised as the other. Meanwhile, interlacing his fingers with mine, Colin leaned against my side. He rested his arm on mine, his elbow in the crook of my own.

"All right," he repeated. "Now help me upstairs."

"You could do it on your own, couldn't you?"

"No, I can't. After all, it's your fault if I'm hurt."

That's how he punished me. In front of Bruce Conway.

On Monday morning I found myself face-to-face with the redoubtable Melanie of the Schmidt Gallery. After discovering that it was I who had sent her the flowers, she would not leave my side. I visited the basement under her protection.

"It's nice, isn't it?" she asked with a broad smile.

"What's nice, the basement or the paintings?"

"The whole thing."

"Yes, it's very nice."

I took the opportunity to study Grindling Conrad's paintings again.

"Did you notice? Your flowers are still fresh. I put them on the table by the entry."

"Ah? So much the better. Tell me, will Miss Fairchild be coming in this morning?"

"That would surprise me."

I tapped my lips nervously with the tip of a finger.

"I hope there'll be a good crowd."

"Oh, no problem. There always is."

"You'll see to it that they don't linger over the horrors upstairs."

"Certainly." She laughed, offhandedly slipping her arm through mine. "You find her attractive—Florence Fairchild?"

"What?"

"Oh, come on now! Don't play the innocent."

"To tell the truth, we get into an argument each time we meet."

"Hmm . . . that I'd really like to see."

"I've sworn to myself I'd stay polite this evening. I have no desire to spoil everything."

"I'll be honest with you, Miss Fairchild gets on my nerves."

"I'm not surprised. And Sigmund?"

"Sigmund? He's crazy about her."

"Oh? Are they sleeping together?"

"I've no idea. But that's not her style. Much too well brought up. . . . Since you mentioned Sigmund Schmidt, I'll let you in on something else. He's convinced he has you in his pocket and that you'll be indebted to him from here on out."

"He's in for a disappointment, poor fellow."

"Hmm . . . you're the terror of this outfit, Mr. Tuncurry."

"Really?"

"Yes. You're always right there with the quick jab."

"Not for you, my dear, not for you."

"If you were to ask me out for dinner, I'd fall for your charms, quite positively."

I thought of Vanessa, to whom I had sent an invitation and with whom I had intended to finish out the evening. "Dinner I cannot. But lunch, if you like."

"I'm on duty today."

"Then we'll do duty together. I'll bring you in a hamburger from the corner."

"With french fries."

"Got it. And a strawberry milk shake. It will be madly romantic."

"And if I should take you at your word?"

"But I'm altogether serious."

"That's good."

And that's how I was picked up by Melanie, to the tune of a Big Mac and a Coke.

At the stroke of three I went home to change. On impulse I put on brown suede trousers, my silk rep shirt of the same color, and desperately searched for a jacket to go with it. Finding none, I settled for a maroon sweater that I draped carelessly across my shoulders. Though I was still pale, with that peculiar glint in the eyes, I no longer looked as though I had just risen from the grave. On the contrary, my emaciated face and my dark, tousled locks completed a look I found quite fetching. Whistling to myself as I locked the door, I drew an echo from the fifth floor.

"Ahoy there! Could this be a recycled rock star?"

"What're you doing there, Conway?"

"I'm taking the air on my doorstep," he replied. "Any law says I can't?"

I leaned on the balustrade, the better to see. "I thought you were working?"

He flinched, then burst out laughing. "Got sacked the second day."

I breathed easier. "On what grounds?"

"I asked them who I should see about joining the union."

"That did it?"

"Not exactly. It was when I called the head of personnel a slimy pig. That's what really did it."

"And now what're you going to do?"

"Dunno . . . but I've really got to find some job. Otherwise it'll be disaster. Sharon doesn't have a whole lot of dough, either."

At the name of Sharon we both stiffened, suddenly on the defensive.

"But what kind of work would you like?" I asked.

"Don't know. I'm not much good at anything." With a shrug he huddled down behind the balusters. Catching a hint of distress in his eye, I was profoundly shocked.

I looked at my watch, then muttered reluctantly, "I'm going to be late."

"Where're you going?"

"To a gallery opening." I hesitated. "Want to come along?"

"Hey, yeah! Great!" Then he sobered. "Ah, no. I can't."

"Why?"

"I've got to go pick up Anita at school. Then Sharon will be worried if I'm not in."

"Leave a note."

"Why, sure . . . but the kid?"

"Damn!" I said, exasperated. "They're nothing but a bother, those two."

"Foster! Leave it alone!"

"But it's true." I let out a sigh. "Bruce, I do have to run. I'll talk to you later."

As I started downstairs Bruce called out to me again. "Maybe we could take her along?"

"Who, Anita?"

"Yeah."

"Get serious, Conway. You think I'm crazy enough to lug that little brat to an art show?"

And that's how I happened to find myself heading for the Schmidt Gallery with Bruce Conway and Anita Dowd. Anita was beside herself at the idea of being my date; she even insisted on wearing her best dress. She wanted to do me honor, particularly after telling me I looked like Peter Pan. (Though I really don't see why, she insisted that we call her Wendy.)

I made them promise to behave, not to touch the paintings with greasy fingers, and to say please and thank you at appropriate moments.

"My, how handsome!" said Melanie the instant she caught sight of me. From the look on Florence Fairchild's face, I concluded that she thought the same.

"Ladies . . ." I bowed ceremoniously.

"Me, too, I'm handsome too," crowed Bruce Conway, rocking back and forth in his running shoes.

"These are friends of mine, Bruce Conway and Anita."

"Wendy!" she corrected me, tugging at my hand.

"Ah, yes, for this evening it's Wendy."

Florence Fairchild's dark eyes flickered from me to Anita by way of Melanie.

"Oh, Daddy, look. There's stuff to eat!"

"Daddy?" The two women expressed surprise in unison.

"Pay no attention," I rejoined. "It's a habit of hers to call the neighbors Daddy."

128

"Oh, but Foster." Bruce chuckled. "I can assure you that you have the exclusive honor."

"Splendid. And now, Captain Kangaroo, how about seeing to Wendy. The buffet is open." I passed my adoptive daughter over to him and gave them both a shove.

"It's not a good idea to put the bar here on the street level," I remarked somewhat nervously. "Everyone's going to congregate here, and they'll never get downstairs."

"There isn't any room downstairs," said Melanie. "We had no choice."

I turned toward Florence Fairchild. "And how are you?"

"As well as possible, given the present company."

"Oh, come, come . . . I'm determined to be agreeable and smiling for once."

"That's why you've already begun to gripe about the buffet table?"

I bit my lower lip pensively. "But you have to admit that I'm right. They'll get to drinking and gossiping, and they won't even look at the paintings."

"That's the way you believe it always goes, right? So what's the difference?"

"True, openings are good for the social columns only."

A rumble of male voices suddenly swept over us. James Coventry and his young lieutenants from the *Review* were vying for loudest. "Already drunk?" I inquired.

"Hi there, buddy!" James gave me a friendly pat on the shoulder before answering. "No, I assure you, not a drop has passed our lips. Matter of fact, I'm dry as a chip."

Florence Fairchild was standing by stiffly, haughty to the tips of her fingers.

"Greetings, fair ladies," said James good-naturedly.

The lovely Florence was getting more and more on my nerves. As I restrained myself with difficulty, Melanie gave me a sympathetic wink. Then she noticed Jerry, who was staring at her like a cat at a goldfish. And at that instant I had the incomparable pleasure of witnessing the first impact of love at first sight. Let's not mince words, it was devastating. Forgotten were poor Tuncurry, art galleries, all the Miss Fairchilds and insolvent art reviews. We watched, totally dumbfounded, while they strolled away together.

"Well, look here, buddy!" James commented, summing it up for all of us.

"I hope Mr. Conrad gets here soon," said Florence Fairchild, finally reacting to the surprising turn of events and attempting to wipe it out of her mind as quickly as possible.

"Because you believe he is going to come?"

"Mr. Coventry, just what are you insinuating?"

"It's not exactly his style. He doesn't generally make the effort."

"Foster!" she turned to me, panic-stricken. "He wouldn't do that to us?"

"How would I know?" I let her suffer for one little moment before going on. "Don't worry, he'll come, I guarantee."

While James Coventry drew his colleagues toward the punch bowl and the wine, I asked Florence whether she had received my roses.

"It seems you send flowers to all the unattached ladies in the neighborhood. I don't feel particularly flattered." She ogled Melanie's bouquet, which was still holding forth by the door.

"You're quite right to count yourself among the unattached." Upon which I went off to join Bruce Conway and Anita. The latter literally leapt into my arms.

"The interesting part is in the basement," I remarked, noting Bruce's obviously perplexed reaction to the circles and triangles.

I was still carrying Anita, who had flung an arm around my neck, to Bruce's vast amusement.

"After you, Daddy," he said.

Down we went. All on her own, Anita pointed to the painting called *Harlequin Betrayed*. "It's a marionette!"

"Yes, if you like."

As for Bruce, he lingered longest in front of *Saint George and the Dragon*. "This is stu-pendous!"

"That's pretty inspired criticism," I rejoined.

"Oh, give me a break, Foster." Then he dug me in the ribs with his elbow, and I recognized the friend I used to know. I suddenly caught sight of Grindling Conrad. Trailed by the faithful Bruce, I went up to him.

"Hello, Tuncurry. You're looking much better than the last time I saw you."

"That's for sure."

Anita suddenly gave me a sneak-attack kiss. "My children like the paintings very much," I said, tilting my head toward Bruce. "Two of my friends, Bruce Conway and Anita."

"Wendy!"

"Ah, yes, Wendy. And just between you and me, I'm Peter Pan."

Grindling Conrad decided to smile. "You're an odd one, you are!"

"Not so bad yourself," said Bruce.

"In appearance, perhaps. But I'm an extremely simple man, a rustic. Rather lightly roughed out; in fact, pretty much in the raw state. But you, Tuncurry, you're an ivory medallion, finely worked, almost like lace or Chinese porcelain. Incredibly complex."

"Enough, enough!" I protested.

"He's quite right," Bruce said, going one better. "Incredibly complex and totally useless."

"He's pretty," piped Anita, who had largely caught the lacy side of the comparison.

"The women found you irresistible," Bruce whispered in my ear, gently rocking from one foot to the other.

"The rest rooms are upstairs," I parried, managing to keep him still for all of five seconds.

"Okay," he said, doing a little dance step toward the stairs. "I wouldn't mind munching on a cracker or two."

We followed him. I was still carrying Anita, which allowed me to avoid shaking hands with Sigmund Schmidt, whom I encountered with Ms. Fairchild at his side.

"Ah, our good friend!" he exclaimed. "Such a cunning little girl! What's your name, treasure?"

To my joy Anita ignored him completely. Grindling Conrad seemed amused. Upstairs, as the guests began trickling in, I was horrified to see Mrs. Ariboska and her flowered hat. Over in the corner, Bruce was consuming everything he could.

"Hoyo!" bellowed Mrs. Ariboska, throwing herself at me as if I were her favorite rock star. "Mr. Tuncurry!"

I mumbled an unintelligible response.

"But what do I see here? Oh, the gorgeous little trinket! Will you tell me your name? Do you go to school? Do you study hard? Are you good to your mommy and daddy? What a beautiful dress! What is your name? Do you go to school?"

Had she even felt inclined to answer, Anita would not have been able to get in a word.

"The show is a complete success," she went on without so much as blinking. "These works are so original! Anyway, Sigmund—Sigmund Schmidt—told me all about them when we lunched together, and he had me convinced in advance. The colors are well chosen, don't you think?"

"The paintings in question are in the basement."

"In any event," she went on without hearing me, "Sigmund—Sigmund Schmidt—declared that he would be the most important painter of our generation."

"Mine, not yours. . . ."

"Do you love your daddy?" she concluded sharply.

"He's not my father," Anita calmly replied.

Mrs. Ariboska looked at me, wide-eyed and uncomprehending.

"They're nice at this age," I said by way of closing as I turned my back on her.

Beginning to feel a slight thirst, too, I joined Bruce at the bar. I put Anita down and gave her a glass of ginger ale, helping myself to a sort of planter's punch that wasn't too heavily laced.

"Everything's okay? You're settling in?" I asked Bruce, who was bolting down his umpteenth cracker, thickly spread with pâté.

"Yum . . . not bad, that one. Here, try some."

He held out some pâté, which I passed over to the kid, who was whining that she wanted a sample too.

At that moment, seeing Vanessa Poretski at the door, I left my two monsters together stuffing their faces.

"Good evening, Vanessa."

"Hello, Foster. My, you're looking chic."

"Thank you. Come, I'll show you what there is to see. I forbid you to look at anything here, you'll get the wrong impression." I took her by the hand and led her along. As we went by, Bruce Conway winked and fell into line behind me with Anita. At the foot of the stairs I found the Schmidt-Fairchild clan just where I had left them, and poor Grindling, who seemed to have sunk to the depths of boredom. The moment he caught sight of me, his face lit up and he hurried over.

"Here's Grindling Conrad. Grindling, Vanessa Poretski."

Then I immediately realized I had just committed the prime error of my love life.

"Ah? This is your lady friend?" Grindling asked.

"Uh . . . no."

Vanessa glanced at me suggestively but refrained from comment.

"Very well. In that case you can have no objections if I spirit her away?"

"Wha—? Uh, no . . ."

Slipping her arm through Grindling's, Vanessa stuck out her tongue at me. "All's fair, Casanova!"

"Peter Pan," Anita corrected her gravely.

"Damned if you didn't miss out on that one," Bruce remarked with a snap of the fingers. Then he burst out laughing at my crestfallen expression. The worst part, however, was catching the eye of Florence Fairchild, who had missed none of it. The arch of her eyebrow did not augur well.

"How about a move back to the bar," Bruce suggested. "At least you could get drunk."

So we returned for a few supplementary glasses. Again I was assailed by Mrs. Ariboska.

"My good friend! The show is a huge success, isn't it? Such a flair for color." She turned to Anita. "Well, now, my little sweetie, are you having a good time? Such a pretty dress!"

Bruce Conway, evidently dumbfounded, was staring at her. Then, to my great joy, he decided to have a little fun.

"My dear, what a fan-tas-tic hat!" This caught her attention.

"Isn't it? Thank you. The exhibition—"

"—is a huge success," he concluded for her. "Such reds! Ah, and this blue! Have you ever laid eyes on a blue that's so . . . so blue?" Then he drooled some of his punch down his front and wiped it up with his sleeve.

An unfortunate waiter was called over and abruptly relieved of his platter of small pastries. Handing me the plate, Bruce proceeded to eat up the sweets, row by row, one every ten seconds. Mrs. Ariboska, entranced, could not take her eyes off the alarming shuttle motion of his arm. Several people gathered to watch, among them Florence Fairchild, who was clearly appalled. James Coventry and his photographer were bent over double, but certainly they were the only ones. Reaching the end, Bruce gulped down the last pastry and belched.

"A little something to drink would be nice. . . . The show
is a huge success, don't you think? Ah! Such a pretty, pretty
yellow!"

He picked up a glass of white wine off the bar and bit into a
cracker spread with cheese.

"Not to be believed," blurted James, and he went off again
into transports of laughter.

Florence Fairchild came toward me, her lips pursed. "From
what I can see, your friends are cut from the same cloth as
you."

Bruce moved back to my side. She cast him an icy look that
turned to smiles as she remembered something.

"Fortunately women are more sensitive than men. You had
a little difficulty with that charming young woman a moment or
so ago?"

"Who? Him?" asked Bruce, throwing an arm around me.
"The very idea!" Then he smirked. "Come on now, Tuncurry
isn't interested in women! What d'you suppose we're doing
here together?"

Florence Fairchild recoiled involuntarily.

"That's the way it is, Florence," I added. "I'm simply not
available."

"Gays and little girls, that's all he wants. Eh, Wendy? Who
is it you call Daddy?"

"Him." She touched me with the tip of her finger.

"But that isn't your real daddy, is it?" Bruce wouldn't stop.
"No . . . no."

"He's nice to you, right? Who got you dressed to come
here?"

"Daddy?" Anita glanced at me with uncertainty, not really
knowing what she should say.

"You're both absolutely revolting!" Florence stated. "After
all I've done for you," she couldn't help throwing in.

"For me?" I retorted. "But you haven't done a thing for me.
You know, Florence, I firmly intended to be civil and agreeable
to you. It's just that your attitude rubs me the wrong way. For
now, maybe my friends and I should leave. To limit the damage. I imagine Sharon would be glad to have her daughter back
by now," I added for Bruce's benefit as we moved away.

"Yeah," he responded phlegmatically. "At any rate, it's almost time for dinner."

I mopped my damp brow. "Are you a bottomless pit?"

"These little snacks always whet my appetite."

"I'm going to say goodbye to Grindling. Wait for me outside." I left in search of Grindling Conrad and Vanessa, whom I found deep in animated conversation.

"So there you are," he said.

"I'm taking my pair of children home and going straight to bed."

"Going to bed?" asked Vanessa.

"Exactly. My legs are like rubber, my head's spinning, I'm exhausted, and everything is going blurry."

"Tell me, have you seen a doctor?" Grindling asked solicitously.

"Advise him rather to see a psychiatrist." I spun on my heels, hearing Florence Fairchild's voice.

"What are you? My shadow?" I inquired hotly.

"But there was goodwill behind my suggestion," she replied. "The more I think of it, the more I believe that you're fundamentally unbalanced."

"Fuck off." Bruce Conway was standing straight as a rod, his fists clenched and looking over the top of our heads in a disturbing manner. It was true that he knew what might really be going on in my brain.

"But I—" Florence began.

"Shut up!" Bruce slipped his arm under mine and drew me off toward the door, where Anita was waiting patiently.

"Don't worry," I mumbled. "I'm okay."

And just as I said it, I felt something akin to vertigo. "Rachel . . ."

"What?" asked Bruce.

I stopped, struggling to keep things and people from waltzing around my head.

"You're looking awfully pale, Foster. Come on, I'll try to get a cab."

"You know, I heard the vertebrae snap. . . ."

"Don't talk."

"But you know that . . ."

"Yes, Colin told me." A strong hand seized my wrist as I staggered.

"I'm going to help you," Grindling offered.

"Are you sick like the last time?" asked Anita, catching hold of my belt buckle.

"We need a cab," Bruce repeated.

"There's always my car."

I pulled myself together and shoved them all away. "No thank you, Ms. Fairchild, I don't need your car. Anyway, I'm fine now."

"Is this a good idea?"

"Sure it is, Bruce, I assure you. I was simply drained. It's the kind of thing I haven't been able to take since—" I bit my lip, failing to choke back a sob. "Let's get out of here."

We began walking again, leaving behind more than one worried or surprised individual. The fresh air immediately did me good. I insisted on setting off for home on foot.

"It's a long way," grumbled Bruce.

Our arrival back at Stairway C was a real pleasure.

"I've been waiting here for hours!" bellowed Sharon Dowd the moment she caught sight of us.

She had left her door open so as to be sure not to miss us.

"And what about Anita? What time will she get to bed tonight? Bruce, we made a definite agreement that—"

"Drop it!"

"Bruce, that's not the way it's going to be. There are certain things we laid down, and you swore you would carry out your obligations. And it's not because I—"

"Stop! This isn't the time."

"Oh, no? And why not?" she insisted.

"I'm taking Foster up to his place."

"He can manage one flight on his own. And anyway, Mr. Tuncurry, I'll thank you to leave Bruce alone. He's got better things to do than waste his time in art galleries. What were you up to all day? Did you look for a job?"

"Uh . . . no."

"Really, Bruce!"

"Do stop!" I implored, in misery. "Don't fight, please."

"Might one ask the reason for all the commotion?" said Beatrice, opening her door right next to Sharon's.

"For once it's not you that's giving someone hell," retorted Sharon disagreeably.

"Foster," exclaimed Beatrice, "you don't look well at all. Come on in and I'll make you a good pot of Chinese tea."

"Good idea. Why don't you clear out."

Beatrice cast an icy look at Sharon. "As for you, I'd advise you not to be rough on my friend Foster, or you'll have a score to settle with the Holt-Sparks."

Taking me by the hand, she led me into her apartment.

"Go on, don't mind her," she said soothingly. "She has a whole mess of problems to deal with herself, poor thing."

She pushed me gently toward an armchair and put on some Berlioz to calm me. Eyes half-closed, I listened to the familiar words of Gautier.

> How bitter is my fate, how bitter is my fate,
> Ah, loveless, setting off across the sea, setting off
>   across the sea . . .

A quick shudder passed over me as I heard,

> And the phantom . . .
> murmurs, reaching out toward me,
> "You shall return."

Beatrice poured me some Lapsang Souchong, and I forgot to

> . . . listen to the turtle dove
> singing on the yew's top branch
> its plaintive chant.

9. *The other guy's the crazy one*

My doctor had prescribed calcium, quantities of magnesium, and also a tranquilizer, which I'd passed up until then. I forced myself to take some, hoping it might bring me out of the temperamental bog that was alternately sucking me in and spewing me out.

I lacked the strength to tackle the wall of incomprehension at the Israeli Consulate once more. I stayed home behind closed doors, emptying the kitchen shelves and spending most of the time zonked out on the sofa. I didn't even go downstairs for the mail and refused to open the door for Colin or Beatrice. I took the phone off the hook.

My sole companion was an endless dealing out and turning over of playing cards in a mindless solitaire.

"If I don't win this time, I'll throw myself out the window."

Naturally I lost that hand and sent the whole thing packing in a fit of rage. Things simply couldn't keep on like this.

I put on a sweater, because I always felt cold. Finally I decided to go out for some food.

The first person I saw was Sharon Dowd. We stared at each other without a word, equally embarrassed.

"Hello," I said in a low voice, almost hoping not to be heard.

"Hello, Mr. Tuncurry." She went past and on up the stairs toward the fifth floor.

"Bruce is in?" I asked abruptly.

"I suppose so." She turned back toward me. "There's no way to make him get up and go look for a job."

"May I? I'd like to come along with you."

137

It was quite clear that this did not enchant her in the least. Nonetheless I doggedly followed her. Her expression alone conveyed her opposition. She and Bruce must have exchanged angry words on my behalf, I supposed, and he had more or less convinced her to spare me. Sharon opened the door with her keys.

"Mr. Conway," she called out, "you have company."

Then she went to sit down, visibly hostile and disapproving. Bruce peered out of the kitchen, a pot in hand.

"I'm coming, Foster. I'm just finishing this."

"What are you making?" I followed him in order to be alone with him.

"Fudge."

I shrugged.

"It's good, fudge is," he insisted. "So, you've decided to poke your nose out of doors?"

"Yes, as you see."

"Colin's been looking odd these days. I think he was almost considering dynamiting your digs so's to know what you were up to, barricaded in there. I bet you didn't knock on his door?"

"No, you're right."

He began to chuckle as he spread his fudge on a buttered plate. "Okay, I just have to pop this into the fridge. . . . Aside from that, my friend, was there something you wanted to tell me?"

"First of all, I'd like Sharon to stop giving me a bad time."

"Ah, well, pal, just whose fault is that?"

"Next, I thought you intended to grow up. All this doesn't seem headed in the right direction."

"Oh, no." He looked at me askance. "Not you too."

"What you need is a job that suits you. Work that would keep you on the move."

"What are you suggesting? Messenger?"

"Hell, why not? It wouldn't be so bad."

"Please don't you worry about me. In this building there are already too many people who're wishing me well!"

"Look, I know perfectly well that you don't give a damn, but I'm forgiving your debts to me."

"That's really nice of you, but could I borrow fifty?"

"God almighty! You'll never change."

"I'm afraid you may be right."

"How can you expect to take on a family?"

"As it happens, it's the family that's taken *him* on," said Sharon, leaning against the door frame.

"Yes, so it seems," I agreed. "It doesn't look to me as though your affair is going anyplace."

"Couldn't I be a man about the house?"

"It would be fine as long as I earned enough, but that's far from being the case."

"What do you do?" I asked her.

"I'm a medical secretary. I can't complain, but my salary won't support three. And, anyway, I'm sick of depriving myself. Just like everyone else, I'd like to buy myself a new dress every now and then, or go to the movies and art galleries. Ever since I was sixteen I've been slaving away. I'm killing myself trying to bring up my daughter well. I've really nothing to apologize for, Mr. Tuncurry, but I, too, would like to whoop it up a bit on Saturday night or argue about music and literature until three in the morning. Only the thing about it is, I can't. Over the weekend I sleep, because I'm too tired to do anything else. I know it's of no interest to anyone, but what I'd like is to work half-time, take care of Anita, take her to the zoo, read to her, take some courses. . . . If it goes on like this, I'll never be able to. I always seem to land guys who need me more than I need them."

"It's not easy to find work right now," Bruce said after a pause.

"No, particularly when you're not looking. And then, you had one, but—"

"We're not going back over that. Incompatible views do exist."

"The problem is, it'll be the same thing each time."

Sharon went back into the living room, apparently angry but perhaps quite simply discouraged. I was still with Bruce.

"She's not altogether wrong."

"I know that," he mumbled wretchedly.

"Suddenly I'm hungry." I changed the subject. "I must admit that with what I've been eating these days . . ."

"Go sit down if you like. I'll bring you a sandwich."

"Milk and cornflakes—that sounds good."

"I'll see if we have any."

I went back and sat down on the sofa in the living room with

Sharon. Agamemnon jumped into my lap, purring. I didn't think to protest. Glancing at her watch, Sharon stood up.

"I'm going to pick up Anita at her friend's house."

"See you later," responded Bruce, bringing in a bowl and glass for me.

"I haven't eaten any solid food for quite some time," I explained, catching Sharon's eye. She made no reply as she went out.

Sitting down beside me, Bruce let me enjoy my cereal in peace.

"I should be ashamed," he said. "But I'm the irresponsible type, and I simply don't feel any shame."

I shoved the cat's nose out of my milk glass and slapped the paw that was going for my corn flakes.

"Your situation's getting critical."

"What the hell! Suppose a rich old uncle dies and leaves me something? The trouble is, I don't have a rich old uncle. Admit it, I'm out of luck. Why is it that only rich people inherit more?"

My cereal bowl emptied, I straightened up.

"You leaving so soon?"

"Right now there's nothing I can do for you."

"And my hundred bucks?"

"Fifty."

"Everything goes up. Eighty?"

I took my wallet out of my hip pocket and emptied it on the table.

"Sixty-five dollars," Bruce counted. "You're making a note of it?"

"Why on earth? You don't have any intention of paying me back, do you?"

"No, that's true. The good thing about you is that money doesn't interest you in the least."

"Probably because I have some."

"That doesn't mean anything."

I shook hands with him before leaving, a thing I never do. It was quarter to seven when I went back home. I wandered back and forth between the kitchen and bedroom, undecided. I could hear *The Rite of Spring,* as I did every evening. Colin Shepherd was trying to get my attention. In the bathroom I noticed wet spots on the ceiling. The tub on the fourth floor must be overflowing on purpose. I reluctantly resolved to go upstairs. Scarcely had I rung when he opened the door, leading me to believe that he had been standing right behind it.

"You're flooding me out again."

"Oh, damn. Come in, come in. It's because of the material; the drain must be clogged."

"The material?"

"Yes, I'm washing my bedspread. Or rather, I'm soaking it. Come on in."

The explanation was something of an alibi. I was convinced that the accident had been arranged.

"It's fixed," he said as he came back. "It didn't have time to do much damage."

"I think I'm going to dig into my pocket and buy you another record," I remarked.

"Oh, but I have others!"

"Not so one would notice."

He ignored my dig. "Are things going better?"

"Why, were things going badly?"

"Oh, Foster . . . you—" He broke off and studied his fingernails intently.

"Well, that's that," I began.

"Where're you going?"

"Home. What d'you expect?"

"You in a hurry? It's days since I've seen you and—"

"And so, you miss me?"

"Why, yes. And besides, I worry. Beatrice too. Evidently you don't give a damn."

"Right, I don't give a damn. Everybody has the right to be left in peace now and then, don't they? Am I obliged to put up with my neighbors for days or evenings or nights at a time? Can't you all leave me in bloody peace?"

"You're making too much of it. You were sick, and it's quite normal for us to watch over you, isn't it? And if you should have another attack down there, what then? We're supposed to let you die?"

"That's right, let me die. It would simplify things."

"Oh, yeah?"

"I'm useless. I wonder what I'm doing here."

"Stop talking nonsense. Are you at least taking care of yourself?"

"Taking care of what?"

"Well, your nerves."

"There you go. Say right out that I'm crazy."

"Foster, why must you twist everything?"

"Well, since you're so interested, you might as well know that I've got heaps of tranquilizers, and I don't know what's keeping me from guzzling the whole lot of them at once. Farewell, problems; farewell, neighbors."

"Oh, shut up, I can't stand that sort of stupidity."

"Very well, you won't have to endure it any longer. I'm going."

"Oh, sit still for chrissake!"

We sat there in silence for a moment, each avoiding the other's eye.

"Foster." He picked up the thread again. "There's something you're not willing to say, and it's driving you bats. Why not trust someone? Why will you never confide in anyone? Is it as difficult as all that? What is the secret that's punishing you, obsessing you, that'll wind up destroying you if you keep on this way? Foster, why do you never share anything personal and important?"

"There are secrets that don't belong to you."

"You're lying."

"I'm the only judge of that. It's up to me to resolve my problems."

"But you're not getting anywhere."

"Oh, yes, I am."

"You frighten me."

"I've simply been surviving. Perhaps at long last I will begin to live." I laughed at the irony. "My existence is conjugated entirely in the passive mode."

"To love is an active verb."

I had no adequate answer to that. Drawing a deep breath I decided to give another try at defining my feelings. "What set the whole thing off was a sudden awareness of reality. I felt real. Physically. How can I explain it better than that? Imagine that you've just run a very great distance at an incredible rate of speed. When you stop, everything is spinning around you, you can't feel your legs, you pant, the oxygen you gulp down knocks you silly, you feel as though you're floating. And then, leaning against a tree, you're there again and you're real. Do you understand?''

"I'm trying.''

Was I even sure myself about what I was trying to express? It was annoying, not being able to make myself clear. And yet everyone seemed to consider me an intelligent being. So where did that leave me?

"My words can't accurately translate my emotions, my pain. Ah, how much clearer thoughts are than words.''

"Go on.''

"I believe that for the first time I've finally been in sympathy, deep sympathy . . . with a dead woman.''

Colin's lower lip twitched, an involuntary indication of disgust. But I couldn't exactly determine the thoughts behind it.

"Is *that* your secret?''

"No. Together with something else, it makes up a whole. How to define it? A test. Yes, that's the word. The whole thing is a test.''

"This is like a charade. My first is a madman. My second . . .''

"If you like. But I see it as a promontory that must be rounded in a storm before reaching calm waters.''

"You aren't even close to resolving it yet, Foster.''

"But I'm not giving up. Knowing that much places me one step toward victory. And then there's also Stairway C and . . .'' I massaged my forehead with a cold hand, exhausted. "Talking is such an effort,'' I added. "You've no idea what fatigue it causes.''

"I'll make you some tea.''

"Tea again,'' I said, smiling.

"I thought you liked it.''

"I do. I've been living on tea for several days running.''

"I can give you something else if you like.''

"No, absolutely not. Tea will be just fine. . . . The tea plant, divine tree born of Bodhidharma's eyelids . . . just what I need.''

"You do have a bit of divine illumination, after all.''

"True. In another era I'd have been exorcised. Particularly with my attacks. Possessed by the devil. These days people go to the psychoanalyst. At times I think perhaps it would be better to fall back on a good old exorcism.''

I relaxed comfortably in the corner of the sofa. Colin disappeared into his kitchen, leaving me alone for a few mintues. I was pleased with myself. Finally I had managed to explain myself, even if clumsily, and the fact of having once more found the way to analyze and criticize myself put me back on firm footing. I was no longer in the grips of insurmountable, destructive terror. The pain was all that was left.

"Here you go, disciple of Zen, the brew of your god."

"As it happens, the actual brew of my god is dago red. You have to admit that it packs more of a wallop."

"Don't blaspheme."

"Oh, come on. I'm not entirely sure about God the Father, but I'm convinced that the Son had a sense of humor."

Sitting across from me, Colin relaxed again into that curious smile I knew so well. At those moments his eyes always stared off into space, making me uneasy. He picked up a cigarette and began to smoke. His face took on the look of Renoir's little girls, a very distasteful notion. Then I thought of Fragonard's little boy with a white dog. And Leonardo da Vinci's *St. John the Baptist* had the same gentleness about the lips and Gainsborough's *Blue Boy* the same dignity. I decided it was ridiculous to compare him to anything at all.

"Why are your pupils expanding and contracting?" he suddenly asked.

"What? I have no idea. Because I was thinking, I guess."

"Thinking about what?"

"Nothing," I lied.

"Liar!" He shrugged.

"I was thinking about Gainsborough."

"I see. Why?"

"Just because . . . Listen, I'm tired."

"Then go home to bed."

"I've done nothing but sleep for two weeks now. It's all those fucking tranquilizers too."

"Hey, could I show you something?"

"Sure, what?"

He stood up and went to leaf through his folders of drawings. He drew out a medium-size sheet.

"Here."

It was a portrait of me.

"Obviously I did it from memory," he added.

I looked it over, not really very pleased. The resemblance was strong, but there was something that bothered me acutely. I couldn't figure out what.

"You don't like it?" he asked anxiously.

"No."

"I should never have shown it to you," he said with a catch in his voice. "I should have known."

"It's well drawn, but . . ." Suddenly I understood. It was me, *before*.

"I'm not like that anymore," I remarked. "See? This isn't me any longer. I mean, look at that expression of self-complacency, that air of certainty, that egotistical look. Is that the way my face looks now? It's not the *same,* is it?"

"Ah . . . yes, you're right."

"Preserve it carefully, it's an historical artifact. Aside from that, you're gifted."

"But Mr. Tuncurry, I'd like to remind you that I've studied art."

"At your age, you should still be in school."

"I'm older than I seem."

"Sure, twelve, or maybe thirteen."

I rested my head on the back of the sofa and breathed deeply. Without a sound Colin came to sit down beside me.

"You're sure you have nothing to tell me, Foster?"

I sat up straight and raised my cup. I took several sips, my eyes on the teaspoon.

"Well, then?" he insisted.

"I don't think so, no."

"I see," he said dryly.

"What more do you want to know?"

"Nothing. Nothing at all."

I was growing impatient. "What does that mean?"

"Nothing important."

He crossed his arms and began to sulk openly. That sort of behavior never failed to surprise me, but it was dangerously effective, for I couldn't long endure it.

"Hey, that's enough. Stop it."

"You really have nothing to say?"

I bit my tongue. One day it would have to come out.

"I apologize," I mumbled.

I could feel the flush on my cheeks, making things even

more painful. Colin let out a deep sigh of satisfaction and stretched.

"Good," he concluded.

Before going home, I rang Virgil's bell. Beatrice asked me in and offered me some tea—she too—but I'd had quite enough. "No, thanks," I replied. "I've just had some at Colin's."

"Aha, so you were at his place. Good. So make yourself at home, my friend. There, relax in the armchair."

"I'm not staying. I just came by to let you know how I'm doing."

"What do you mean? Surely you don't have the gall to refuse dinner at the Sparks'?"

"Oh, well, if you're inviting me, that's a whole other matter. Virgil isn't here?"

"He's in the shower, the angel."

"Ah, yes, his semiannual ablutions."

"You said it. He's a corporeal cleanliness maniac. His water bills are twice as high as the electricity."

We were still laughing when Virgil made an appearance, a towel girding his loins.

"Oh, so it's you. I was wondering if Beatrice was talking to herself."

"Go get some clothes on, you clown!" she retorted. "He's skinny, don't you think?"

"You cut that out! Would you rather I had a beer belly?"

He went into the bedroom, grumbling that he was not skinny, but that he certainly had fair skin.

"He's nice—a bit stupid but nice," said Beatrice, following his receding form with benevolence. Perching on the arm of my chair, she gave me a tap on the thigh.

"And so, Foster, old pal, are things going more to your liking?"

We talked until around two A.M., when I made a move to leave.

"You don't have to go yet," Beatrice pleaded.

"Yes, I do, or you'll never get rid of me."

"He's quite right. Get your ass out of here, Tuncurry!"

"Hey, Virgil! That's rude," declared Beatrice.

"But he's the one who wants to go. And, anyway, I have an idea or two about ways to spend the rest of the evening. . . ."

"We're wondering what they might be." Beatrice nodded gravely.

"I'd feel guilty if I kept you any longer." I slid crab-wise toward the door. "I bid you a fond farewell," I quipped as I left.

Letting myself in my own door, I realized that oddly, I wasn't tired in the least.

The next morning I woke up with the distinct impression I'd forgotten to do something. After consulting my bedside clock, I concluded that the most important thing I'd omitted was in fact to wake up at a proper hour. So I consumed my breakfast and lunch at one sitting. It was while I was sipping my coffee that I realized what was really bugging me. My phone had been off the hook for several days. I played with it until I got a dial tone, then replaced the receiver in the cradle. When the thing began to ring ten minutes later, I was almost sorry I'd done it.

"Hello," I growled.

"Oh, Foster?"

"Yes."

"This is . . . uh . . ."

"Don't bother, I recognize your voice, Florence. What do you want?"

"I've been trying to reach you for a whole week."

"My telephone was out of order."

"Ever since the opening I've been thinking about you steadily."

"How nice of you."

"Look, Foster. I assure you I feel dreadful about the way I behaved. I feel I hurt you and I—"

"Please don't worry about it. You weren't responsible. I was very sick, that's all."

"But I certainly didn't help."

"I'm not asking you to say that. But it's not important, really."

"So you're not too angry with me?"

"Why, no."

"Then I'm relieved. Guess what—we sold four of Grindling Conrad's paintings."

"Four?" I repeated, flabbergasted.

"Astonishing, isn't it?"

"I must admit I wasn't expecting it. Which ones went?"

"Uh . . . *The Sunken City, Young Girl Bending Over Swiftly Running Thoughts, The Flying Dutchman,* and *The Carnation of Passion.*"

"Great. Is Grindling pleased?"

"Who can tell?"

"Yeah, I know what you mean. Well, at least he didn't refuse to sell them, did he?"

"No, thank God." There was a brief pause. "Uh, Foster . . ."

"Yes," I was quick to reply.

"Do you think we could meet without tearing one another apart?"

"Well, I don't know. . . ."

"Would it be worthwhile giving it one more try?"

"Which is to say?"

"Suppose I ask you for dinner tomorrow night?"

"You're asking me?"

"Yes. At my place, for instance."

"Well, it might please you to know that you've caught me totally by surprise."

"I get the feeling I've misjudged you."

"That's partly my fault."

"Well, then, we'll start from scratch?"

"Gladly."

"I'll come and get you in my car."

"That's too much to ask."

"No, no. It's no bother. And I'd also like to say that, uh . . . last Monday you were terrific."

"Thanks, and I'd say the same for you. It'll be unbearable if we begin exchanging compliments."

"We'll manage. So then, see you tomorrow?"

"See you tomorrow."

I hung up and executed a little dance step. Then I remembered that I had no right to be happy.

I needed to talk with someone else. I went out into the stairway, undecided whether to go up or down. Josh Hardy appeared in the entry and passed me on my doorstep without so much as a word. I couldn't bring myself to say hello.

I was thinking of Grindling Conrad. He was the one who might be able to help me. I'd take my chances. Perhaps I'd find him at home. Deciding as usual not to face the subway, I hugged my Icelandic sweater closer to my ribs and caught a cab.

Twenty minutes later I got out in front of Grindling's building. All the way to the curb from his alley doorway I could hear him singing. His door was wide-open, and I found him stripped to the waist, a scarf tied around his head. He was painting.

"Hello," I said timidly, disturbed at finding him so busy.

He made no answer but kept right on with his work, paying no attention to me. Stepping inside, I looked for the only stool, to sit down. Grindling had placed his paint pots on it. As a last resort, I leaned against the only free wall space.

"Hello," I tried a bit louder.

Grindling made an impatient gesture. "Yeah, I heard you," he groused.

"I didn't mean to interrupt you. I'll go."

He decided to look my way.

"No, don't leave," he said anxiously. His distressed reaction to my testiness astounded me. "Stay right there."

After clearing off the cluttered seat he offered it to me. A futile gesture, actually, because it was still wet from the paint that had dribbled onto it. I preferred to stand.

"Are you cold?" he asked.

I sighed. "All the time."

I went up to the canvas, curious to see his way of going about it. But he immediately stopped me.

"That puts me off," he said straightaway.

Somewhat ungraciously I stepped back. He put the pots back on the stool.

"Florence Fairchild told me that four of your works were sold," I began.

He growled something I couldn't catch.

"You're not pleased?"

"Sure I am. But they set the price too high."

"And you don't like that?"

"They're not worth that much money."

"Really!" I said with a laugh. I'd never met an artist who undervalued his own work.

"It's nothing but scraps of poorly drawn paper," he added as though he were following my thoughts. "What can I do? I simply find folding money so ugly."

"Now that's more like you."

"Why's that?"

"Never doing anything just like everybody else."

"Who, me? I'm very ordinary. You're the one who's odd."

"Ordinary? People panic the moment they see you."

"Exactly. It's more reassuring for others to say 'he's crazy. He paints like a madman.' That's normal. But I'm not mad. That's what's frightening. A well-balanced guy who paints like a madman, that scares them. It's irrational."

"There's something in what you say, I admit."

"Me, I'm simple. You're the one who's complicated."

"How exactly?"

"Why were you so intent on helping me?"

"Because I like what you're doing and want to go to bat for you."

"You must not be very fond of yourself," he remarked. "Letting yourself go this way."

"I'm sick."

"I believe you. But why do battle for me?"

"I believe you're a genius. That was well worth an effort on my part, and I did it."

"No." He dried his brush and placed it in a box, which he shut with great care.

"No, sir, Mr. Tuncurry."

"There, I don't get you."

"You're battling for *yourself.*"

"Okay, I understand what you're insinuating. You undoubtedly imagine that I'm justifying myself, that I'm realizing myself through you."

"Not at all."

Perplexed, I followed his movements minutely. He put the tops back on the paint jars, very gently screwing them tight.

"I'll go back to the beginning of our conversation," he went on. "You're the real nut. But in your mind it's the other guy."

I shook my head, violently denying this.

"Oh, yes, yes," he affirmed. "I serve as a relief, a safety valve for your anxieties."

"I may be cracked," I retorted, "but nonetheless I know what I'm doing."

"No, that's just it. I don't believe you do. If you had thought it over, you would never have asked Schmidt to give me the show. It's simply that you don't want to use your brain anymore. Because you'd come to realize that it wasn't functioning correctly. So, make way for the rest.''

"The rest of what?''

"The epidermis. The skin. And, God Almighty, how pale your skin is!''

"Fine, but what can I do about all this?''

"Accept yourself. Don't pass off on your neighbor the name that's rightfully yours.''

"My neighbor?'' I retorted vehemently.

"It's a figure of speech. I wasn't thinking of anyone in particular. On the other hand, I find it interesting that harmless words get such a reaction out of you.''

I tried to appear relaxed.

"I thought . . .'' I mumbled. "After all, you met Bruce Conway.''

"Yes, you called him your child.''

I'd forgotten that, but it was true. Wasn't that what he was for me? "You're suggesting that I take the label for myself?''

"No, it so happens. There is nothing infantile or innocent about you. But if you'll allow me, avoid that kind of relationship.''

"Which is to say?''

"Sooner or later sons reject their fathers. Beware of what might happen to you with that child.''

"We've already been through our Oedipal crisis,'' I quipped.

Grindling broke off the discussion and offered me a glass of Irish whiskey, which I downed in his fashion, in one gulp. As I left for home, my head was spinning wildly enough to make me regret it.

Reluctantly I was searching my brain for the name I had tagged onto Colin Shepherd. Ah, yes . . . the homosexual, he's the other guy.

10. *Sweet and sour*

I was wandering around the West Village near the docks, when my eyes fell on a help wanted sign. I scanned the building. LUTHERAN CLINIC FOR HANDICAPPED CHILDREN.

Driven by curiosity, I went in. A pretty young woman in a nurse's uniform was filling out forms beneath a portrait of Martin Luther. When I cleared my throat, she looked up.

"Oh, hello," she said very agreeably.

"Hello. I just read the announcement outside and . . ."

"You're interested?"

"Why . . . yes."

"Just a moment, please. I'll call the head of the clinic."

Very soon a middle-aged man appeared. Glancing into every nook and cranny, he approached, at a rather ungainly lope. The moment he reached the reception desk, he began straightening a file folder.

"How do you do," he said with verve. "I am Dr. McCornish."

I introduced myself.

"Would you like to take a tour? I always take people around *before*. The majority leave at a run once they've seen the dormitory for the incurables."

"I'm not here on my own behalf," I explained. "But I have a friend . . ."

"Yes, yes. They all say the same thing—it's never for themselves."

"But it's true, I swear."

"Yes, yes."

Bounding up the stairs, he led me to the next floor.

152

"My friend is a lot like you," I said. "He doesn't stay put
for long in one place, either."

Dr. McCornish stopped to stare at me intently.

I went on. "What kind of help are you looking for?"

He paused, scowling, before he answered. I noticed a tremor
in his right leg.

"First of all, the pay is poor."

"Sure, that figures."

"And then, I only want unqualified people."

"*Un*qualified?"

"Exactly. Children in hospitals are entirely surrounded by
qualified medical personnel. What they need is normal people
who have nothing to do with cures and treatments. That way,
it's as though a member of their own family were with them.
You see? Psychologically it's basic. Anyway, we have noticed
significant progress since we began this experiment. Unfortunately it's usually women who come forward. We lack men,
and that's too bad."

"What sort of work do you have in mind?"

"To eat with the children, play with them, talk, hug them,
kiss them, love them. . . . And it's not easy, take it from one
who knows. Come along."

He opened a door onto a large room containing six beds. In
each one lay a deformed, drooling child. A woman of about
fifty was going from one to another, whispering endearments. I
could scarcely make out human forms. The doctor was watching me intently.

"Rest assured," he stated, "they won't live long. These are
the incurables, and they rarely reach their eighth birthday. Are
you astonished that they need love just like others?"

Shutting the door, he took me on farther where, in a huge
room, ten or twelve children were playing, laughing, shouting,
or crying. A few adults were gaily participating in the uproar. A
little boy with blond hair and dark eyes was sitting stock-still on
a low chair. I went up to him, surprised. The child's beauty
would have given pride to many a mother.

"It's funny," said Dr. McCornish. "Everyone falls for
Paul."

"He's beautiful."

"Yes, isn't he? Everyone thinks so except his parents."

"What does he have?"

"He's autistic."

It wouldn't have taken much for me to spirit him away. Then I remembered that I was in a hospital, not an orphanage.

"Doggie! Doggie!"

A little girl with Down's syndrome was calling with her arms stretched out.

"That's me," said the doctor. "I have the misfortune to be named Douglas."

He left me and went over to kiss the little girl. I quickly found myself accosted by a five- or six-year-old boy who batted me again and again with his teddy bear. I snapped up the toy and hid it behind my back. He stared at me, stupefied, and looked all around. For an instant I shook the plush animal in front of him before hiding it again. He frowned and appeared, much to my chagrin, about to burst into tears. But, no. Instead he walked around me and found his teddy. He burst into laughter as he took it back and began to pound me with it again, to go on with the game. This time, when I grabbed the bear, I tucked it under my jacket. He began to search right away and quickly realized what I had done. His shrieks caught the attention of Dr. McCornish, who came over to stand and watch us.

"You would do all right here," he commented.

"Thanks. But as I already said, it's not for myself that I came."

"Ah, yes . . . well, I forgot. You might give Jonathan a little kiss before we go. He'd be delighted."

Crouching down in front of the little boy, I gave him a kiss and one for his bear, which brought on another wave of piercing shouts. Paul hadn't budged, a stranger to sound and movement. I gazed at him again, fascinated by his immobile face and reflective expression.

"And your friend, will he come?" asked the doctor somewhat ironically.

"I'm just about sure he will."

He closed his eyes in reflection. "We pay by the hour," he said, giving in at last. "And nobody here does more than thirty hours a week, because it's absolutely exhausting. You'll earn—beg your pardon—your friend will earn five dollars an hour. We cannot pay more, though at that our Lutheran benefactors are on the generous side. We offer the widest possible range of hours—seven days a week, twenty-four hours a day."

"Even at night?"

"Certainly. Because of nightmares, particularly."

"I see. While I think of it, do you accept donations?"

"Why? To assuage your guilt?"

"I'm well past that puerile stage."

"That's good. In that case, we accept charity from others."

Soon after that we found ourselves back in the entrance hall facing dear old Martin Luther.

"And will your friend come soon?"

"I hope so. His name is Bruce Conway. You'll easily recognize him. He, too, is always bounding up and down."

"He too?"

"Yes, just like you."

I left a folded check with the young nurse, who repaid me with her most charming smile. Dr. McCornish, not restrained by tact, verified to see that I had drawn it correctly. I then bade farewell to both of them.

"You think so? You really think so?" Bruce Conway cavorted like a young goat, beaming, as he said the same thing over and over. "You think so? You really think so?"

"Yes," I replied for the fifth time. "Now I'm sure there's a place in this world for the hyperactive. When you see Dr. McCornish, you'll have no futher doubts."

"You think so," he concluded.

Sharon had not yet said a word. I could see by her expression that she was not pleased, but I had no idea why.

"And you, Sharon, what do you think of this?" I asked politely.

"What do I think?" She gave a start, surprised to be addressed.

"Yes, you surely must have some reaction."

"This isn't what's going to bring us in real money; that's all I see in it."

Bruce's smile collapsed.

"You don't look at things from the positive angle," I rejoined. "Bruce can't work like everyone else. That's all there is to that. He needs some interest, and he wants to live at his own rhythm. Sure, it doesn't pay a whole lot, but it does pay. The most important thing is that he's finally got something suited to him. Anyway, it's this or nothing, right?"

"But with all his debts, what way is there to repay them? I don't know where we can—"

"I forgave him mine, and I'm sure Colin will do the same. As for the rest of it . . . it should work out, I hope."

I looked at Bruce's gloomy face.

"Well . . ." he began. "I'll put in lots of hours the first week," he finished enthusiastically.

Sharon shrugged, almost scornful in the face of Bruce's lighthearted attitude. That annoyed me.

"Come on, let's see a bit of enthusiasm. How about it? I know Bruce is going to like it at the clinic."

A long, tense silence caught us up.

"Sharon," said Bruce very shyly.

"Okay, I agree. But I advise you to really catch hold this time!" She sighed. "I must be an idiot."

"No, you're not!" Bruce cried out, radiant.

He dropped to his knees in front of her and kissed her hands. Drawing her firmly toward him, he eventually planted a kiss on her lips. I'd never seen him behave amorously in the least. I tried to look elsewhere.

"Sharon, sweetie," Bruce wheedled, "don't you have an urgent need to go buy some cigarettes?"

"What?"

"Please. I have two words to say to this Outer Mongolian standing behind me."

Feigning anger, she pushed him away and stood up. "What have I done to deserve this?" she grumbled on her way out.

Rocking from heel to toe, Bruce was clearly searching for a way to say what he had to say.

"Well, then?" I asked by way of encouragement.

"Well, here it is. . . . I don't understand a single thing about this friend of mine. You see, he's nice to me, he lends me cash, and afterward he wants to hurt me. He does a whole lot of mean things to me, and later he's as nice as you please again, even polite with ladies. I simply don't understand a thing about that friend. How about you? Can you explain him to me?"

"He must be a damn fool."

"No, I don't think so."

"At any rate, he behaves like a fool."

"No, not that, either. . . . There must be some reason behind the things he does."

"Perhaps the friend has been scared."

"By what?"

"By seeing a rational balance suddenly destroyed, a situation changed. He tried to keep things as they were, to keep them from evolving. It's very selfish."

"Ah! That's possible. But he himself changed, didn't he?"

"Fortunately. That's what made him turn nice again, only this time he isn't self-centered anymore. He's trying to take into account the views and wishes of others. Instead of sidestepping them."

"I see. I have a clearer understanding of what happened to that friend."

He turned his marvelous smile on me, and I felt as though I were melting (as they say in romance novels).

"Fine. Now, suppose we were to talk about Colin Shepherd."

"What? Where's the connection?"

"Well, what do you intend to do?"

"What're you talking about?"

"Listen, we're not blind in this building. Even Virgil noticed it—"

"Noticed what?"

"Colin Shepherd."

"Would you kindly make your point?"

"For heaven's sake, Tuncurry! You're not going to pretend you don't know what I'm talking about! Just think it over. Who is it that cares for you tenderly when you're sick? Eh? Who holds your hand in the stairway? Eh? Who invites you in for breakfast? No, no! Take your time before answering. Concentrate. Who . . ."

"To all of that I could answer Beatrice. She takes care of me, takes me by the hand. And Virgil invites me in for breakfast. . . ."

"Give me a break!"

"At any rate, I don't see that it's your business at all."

"Foster, when are you gonna wise up?"

"Wise up to what, asshole?"

"Calm down, calm down. I simply wanted to be sure that you are aware that Colin is in love with you—and that you are going to behave properly for once."

"Properly?"

"Tactfully. I wouldn't want poor Colin to suffer because of you."

"What're you suggesting?"

"Nothing at all, my friend. It's your problem. Only, knowing your gift for doling out abuse, I wouldn't want him to get the brunt of it. He's a delicate figurine. Watch you don't break him."

"Now there, Bruce, baby, you're way off base! If someone's going to get broken, it'll be me. Colin Shepherd may be made of porcelain, but he's un*break*able, that I guarantee! Believe me, I know him better than you do."

"Oh, I've no doubt about that. Now it'll probably enrage you to hear it, but I think you go well together, though I've no idea why."

Quite clearly everyone wanted to push me at Colin Shepherd. I was the only one trying to resist.

"Will you stay for dinner?" Bruce asked.

"I don't think Sharon quite appreciates—"

"No, you're wrong. She has that way of appearing a bit cold, but really, you know, she isn't holding a grudge against you anymore. And then, the little one would really be pleased."

"The . . . thanks a bunch. Oh, shit!" I leapt to my feet and ran for the door.

"But what's the matter, Foster?"

"I forgot, I completely forgot! I'm going out this evening. I've got to dash downstairs or all she'll find is a locked door!"

"She, who?" he asked with great interest.

"Oh, you remember . . . Florence Fairchild."

"That's impossible!"

He looked at me wide-eyed, the model of total stupefaction.

"Well, pal . . . you certainly keep us guessing. And what about her—do you love her?"

"Me? Now how would I know that already?"

He frowned. "Hmm . . . Have a thought for Colin."

"Hey, look here. I do as I see fit, okay?"

"Sure, sure. Still . . ."

"So long, gotta run. See you tomorrow."

I took the stairs two at a time. I dashed into my bedroom to change. Hoping Florence wouldn't arrive in the midst of it, I had half a second to admire myself in the mirror before she rang.

"Good evening, Ms. Fairchild," I said ceremoniously, with an exaggerated Japanese bow.

"Good evening, Mr. Tuncurry," she said with a curtsy.

I drew back to let her in, regretting that I hadn't had the chance to comb my hair. She was wearing a dark pink dress and a black jacket thrown across her shoulders. I paid her a compliment on her beauty, and she returned it in kind. Then we looked at one another uneasily without speaking.

"It's astonishing," she abruptly spoke up. "I simply can't figure you out. Usually one can place people in categories, more or less accurately. But you, really, I don't know."

I offered her a drink before leaving. As she sat on the sofa she asked whether I had a cat. I told her that the rips in the upholstery were due to a beast belonging to my neighbor whom she had met. This brought us around to the topic of the exhibition.

"It went extremely well. Sigmund was delighted. James Coventry promised to do an article for his next issue on the opening, with a lot of photographs. Without costing you a penny it was a thoroughgoing success. How do you suppose they manage to bring out a weekly devoted to art without going bankrupt?"

"Quite simply, because the director has other irons in the fire and can write off the deficit."

"He's a good man, in that case."

"Not altogether, no. But he has a son, Randolph, and it's for him that he makes the sacrifice."

"Well, then, he's a good father, if not a good man."

"Yes . . . I have minor reservations. But no matter."

I sipped my martini. "You undertook some risk in organizing all that in one week," I noted.

"I wanted to show you just what I was capable of doing. You'd been so horrible to me . . . and I to you. But when you smile like that, you're very handsome, Foster."

"Thank you. So this way everyone stands to gain, everyone is happy. And all of it thanks to me, right? And as for me, what do I get out of it? Nothing."

"And what about me?"

"You? You're my consolation prize?"

"Oh, really, Foster, consolation prize—that's a bit much."

"I'm not complaining."

She blushed slightly. Under her outwardly reserved appearance I was sure that she concealed a . . . well, a warm nature.

"Perhaps we could go now if you like," I said, putting down my empty glass.

"Certainly."

On the stairs we passed Colin Shepherd, deep in his mail as he walked up to his apartment.

"Hi, Shep."

Surprised, he looked up but took a moment to answer.

"Oh, hi, Foster." He turned to Florence. "Evening . . . ma'am."

Florence returned his greeting and we went on down. I was conscious that he stopped to watch us leave. Though it bothered me somewhat, it would put him in his place.

"He's charming, your neighbor," Florence commented.

"Yes, he is. Charming and . . ."

On the point of adding "and gay," I fortunately stopped myself in time. First of all, it was none of her concern, and then, I had no right to reduce Colin to a label. Colin Shepherd was, after all, Colin Shepherd in his entirety, with all his virtues and all his faults.

The lovely Florence had a chocolate-colored Mercedes.

"Publicity pays well," I quipped.

"It's a present from my mother," she replied, starting the engine.

"I'm sure."

"Don't be facetious. This *is* from mother. She's a widow, but my father didn't leave us destitute. The apartment where I live belonged to him too."

"Another businessman . . ."

"He had a real-estate firm. My mother still holds some shares, and believe me, she knows how to handle them!"

"Fascinating."

"You're the one who brought it up."

"True. I wanted to know whether this superb machine was a present from Schmidt."

"What an idea! Why?"

"You're not sleeping with him?"

She braked the car hard, throwing me toward the windshield. "I demand an immediate apology!"

"But I wasn't being in the least judgmental. I simply asked a question. You're free to do as you please."

"An apology!"

I gave her a kiss on the cheek, which effectively shut her up. "There," I said softly. "But if you're not sleeping with him, I'm very pleased to know it."

Then, lacking a kamikaze spirit, I buckled my seat belt.

"You're impossible!"

"So it seems. That's why you find me attractive, isn't it?"

With a laugh she put the car in gear again. We started up Third Avenue.

She drove me to a classy neighborhood, to a classy building (even the garage was classy), to a classy apartment.

"This is classy," I said.

"Yes, it isn't bad. I hope you like spicy food."

"Why, did you have it sent up from the corner Chinese deli?"

"Not at all. This comes from the Philippine restaurant. They have excellent food."

"Fine. I adore it. That's perfect. I couldn't dream of better. I'm in perfect bliss."

"Enough of that, monster!"

She gently pushed me toward a chair beside a table set for two.

"You sit down. I'll be back."

As she vanished she called out for me to light the candles. I did so, admiring the perfect romantic setting of yesteryear. The only difference is that then it wasn't the woman who put on the candlelight dinner. She returned bearing an ice bucket containing a magnum of Moët.

"Well, Flo, baby, you certainly don't do things by halves."

She gave me an ironic smile. "As you say . . ."

"And what's on the menu?"

"Sinigang, guinataan, and pinakabet."

"Good thing I asked. Now I know. Which of the three is the dog roasted on a spit?"

"Gag!"

"I thought it was the Philippine national dish."

"Maybe, but it isn't done in New York."

The sinigang turned out to be a sort of fish stew, the guina-taan was pork and vegetables cooked in coconut milk, and the pinakabet a delicious dish of boiled tomatoes and pork, with a fish sauce. The dessert consisted of a kiwi sherbet and some dried mango.

We chatted all through the meal. We took our cardamom coffee in the living room, sitting side by side on the sofa. When Florence wasn't looking, I moved in a bit closer. She gave a start and pushed me back.

"Hey, there! Where do you think you are?"

I pulled back unwillingly.

"Are you angry?"

"Yes," I grouched.

"You'll have to put up with it!"

"But you didn't bring me here for nothing, did you?"

"For nothing? How about the pleasure of my company? That counts for nothing?"

"But that's just it! It is your company I want." I got down on my knees in front of her and took her hand.

"Florence . . ."

"Foster . . ."

I kissed the tips of her fingers, then her palm.

"You seem almost sincere," she said, nonetheless withdrawing her hand from mine.

"But I am sincere."

"Exotic dishes must be aphrodisiacs."

"You don't want to make love with me?"

"Well, quite honestly . . ."

"No?"

"I don't feel so inclined at the moment. When I do, I'll let you know. It's for me to decide, not you."

"You're trying to kill me!" I cried, collapsing onto her knees.

She couldn't keep from laughing but asked me to remove my head from her lap. Sitting up, I pointed to the scar at the corner of my mouth.

"See that, do you? You're the one who did it, the day you hit me with your ring."

"Oh, yes, I remember. You'd been particularly awful that time."

"Might as well warn you right away: I'm going to be a lot more awful if you keep on making fun of me."

She kissed me lightly on that side of my mouth.

"Poor Foster . . . what a name you have."

"It was my father's idea. He always has farfetched ideas."

"To have you for a son was certainly one of them."

Slipping my arm around her shoulders, I toyed for a moment with her thick curls. I drew her in a bit closer and stroked the back of her neck. At first she leaned against me rather stiffly, then melted completely. I gave her a long kiss, then pulled away, gripped by an irrepressible wave of laughter.

"What's gotten into you?"

"Nothing," I said with a gasp.

"What do you mean, nothing?"

"It's ridiculous," I replied, half-choking.

"Philippine cooking definitely doesn't agree with you."

"Oh, yes, it does!"

"What?"

"That's the first time," I explained, "the first time I've ever tasted a cardamom kiss."

Then she laughed too.

"It's not bad, actually. I think I'll even have some more."

Soon after that, we went into her bedroom. Sitting on the edge of the bed, I protested when she made a move to flee into the bathroom.

"I adore the sight of a woman undressing for me. Don't hide."

"I don't enjoy doing a striptease for repressed gentlemen."

I sighed. "You're still being nasty to me." I unbuttoned my shirt. "Look, I'm going to get undressed in front of you."

"You don't have to go on about it."

She disappeared, and I took off my clothes. I turned down the covers, and after providing myself with an ashtray and a pack of cigarettes, I got into bed. While waiting, I lit one. When she reappeared, she was wearing a pink silk nightgown. When I caught her disapproving glance at my cigarette, I hastily put it out.

"I was beginning with the end," I apologized.

When she paused in front of the light, I was able to admire her figure.

"Now you may look."

She let the silky things fall to the floor, revealing what I'd only been able to guess.

"You approve?"

"Now may I handle the merchandise?"

I stretched voluptuously. Florence brushed my chest and face with her mop of curls. When I protested that I couldn't eat, she laughed. Then I polished off the last of the buttered toast and blackberry jam.

"Best little breakfast I've ever had," I stated, pushing the tray to the foot of the bed.

"You might have said something like that to me last night."

"What, for instance? That it was the best lovemaking experience of my life?"

"Just for instance."

"But that would have been a lie."

She raised a hand menacingly. "You cad! Defiler of young womanhood!" She got up, beckoning me to follow her. "I have no desire to take my shower alone."

It was around ten when I got home, dancing and whistling on the stairs. A door on the fourth floor opened instantly.

"Foster?" I saw Colin coming downstairs.

"Hi," I answered gravely.

"You're just coming in now? You spent the night out?"

"No, in. But elsewhere."

"With that woman? Who is she?"

"How could that make any difference to you?" I retorted with a shrug.

He paused a moment. "Well, it does."

"Well, you honestly shouldn't worry about it!"

"Perhaps."

Since I was in a hurry and had no intention of having a scene with Colin over Florence Fairchild, I closed the door. When I had changed and was on my way out again, Colin was sitting on the steps across from my apartment, sulking.

"Where are you going?" His question was half accusation.

"Colin! What's with you?"

"You could give me a simple answer."

"I'm going to the Israeli Consulate, it so happens."

"Oh, that's where she works?"

"Who? Hell, no. I feel like going there for a vacation."

"To the consulate?"

"To Israel, idiot."

"Hey, good idea! Take me along?"

"To the consulate?"

"To Israel, idiot," he said, imitating my tone of voice.

"Not this trip. I'm going alone . . . almost."

"Almost?"

"Someday I'll explain but not now. I'm in a real hurry, no time to chat. So long, see you."

"You're in love with her?"

"Who? Oh, gimme a break!"

Feeling guilty by the time I reached the ground floor, I turned to call back upstairs. "No, I'm not in love with her!"

And I immediately regretted saying it.

On the way I bought a hamburger, knowing I'd have a long wait at the consulate. In fact, it was two-thirty by the time they saw me. It was a different person this time, though, a woman. When I'd given my explanation, she shunted me off to the guy I'd called a fool. I resigned myself to taking him on again.

He didn't immediately recognize me, which gave me cause for mild hope. But after listening patiently through my brief monologue, he clearly recalled the saga. I prayed to heaven he'd forgotten the insult.

"I believe I have already responded to your request," he observed with rancor.

"Yes, I know. But I've . . . how can I put it . . . a moral obligation to persist."

"I said no, and it's still no."

I bit my lip, hard. "I would like to see your superior."

"That's impossible."

"Why?"

"Because he has no time to waste."

"And me, do you think I have?"

"That is hardly my problem."

Furious, I stood up and immediately felt the blood drain from my face. "When I stop to think that I'm not even Jewish and I'm taking on this pile of shit!"

I caught hold of the chair back, for things were beginning to blur. It took me a moment to calm down. The cretin behind the desk undoubtedly had me classified among the screw-loose and other pests.

"I'll send you a postcard when I get to Tel Aviv," was my concluding remark, to which he made no response. I began to get an inkling of the reason why some people might hire hit men. Ah, bureaucracy!

I reached home fuming, discouraged, revolted, and a nervous wreck. After slumping in my armchair for a good long time, I gave way to irrational actions. I took the urn, the photograph, and the bracelet out of the closet. Placing them on my table, I lit two candles and immersed myself in prayer, kneeling there on the ground. Leaning forward, I struck my head against the edge of the table. The blow came as an alarm bell to my deranged faculties. I lifted my head, a little short of astounded to find myself there.

Good God, what was I doing? Had I fallen to the level of fetishism? At all costs I'd have to break these disturbing, obsessive ties binding me to a child's link bracelet and an urn filled with ashes.

I came close to causing a fire as I knocked over the candlesticks in a hasty, awkward move to conceal the magical objects clouding my vision.

In an attempt to escape their fascination I hurried up the stairs to Colin's. Needless to say, the door remained shut to my appeals. I tried Bruce Conway, in vain. The building was empty. I didn't want to return to my own apartment, yet couldn't make up my mind to leave Stairway C, where I felt protected.

I was simply waiting it out on the landing when an idea occurred to me. A while back Colin had given me that duplicate set of his keys for security's sake. So there was nothing to prevent me from going there if I wanted to.

I had just enough courage to go back to my place for the keys, which I'd stashed away in a drawer. At that very moment the phone rang. Something told me I'd better pick it up.

"Hello," I said, surprised by the sound of my own voice.

"Son?"

"Father?"

"Well, hello!"

"But where are you?"

"In Switzerland, of course. I'm calling to alert you."

"About what?"

"That you will have the dubious pleasure of my presence in three days' time."

"Really! You'll be staying in New York?"

"Not for long, unfortunately. You know I can't be away from your mother more than a week. I hope we'll be able to see one another?"

"Of course."

"Unless, that is, you want to use my arrival as an excuse for a sudden weekend away. I'd put that down to your bad filial nature."

"Sounds as though you'd like that."

"I've already renounced you, banished and disinherited you. I'd as soon you gave me cause!"

I laughed, my equanimity suddenly restored. My father had never talked in any other way. In fact, it had turned into a sort of ritual between us. There was a time, when I was still living with my parents, that my father disinherited me at every meal. This always took place before the absolutely imperturbable eyes of my dear mother, who had come to expect it.

"Still there, Foster?"

"Yes, Dad. I'd be very happy to see you. Sincerely."

"Fine. So I'll be seeing you soon, wastrel son!"

"Splendid, unworthy father!"

After our conversation I wondered all over again how my father could ever have chosen diplomacy as a career, he who was so ill-suited to it! In truth, I don't think he gives a damn. It does seem odd, though, to succeed in an area one refuses to take seriously. I subsequently persuaded myself that this is surely the key to success.

But for the moment I sat in my armchair, gazing absently at Colin's keys. Though I no longer felt the need to flee, I still had an urge to see Colin's apartment while he wasn't there. But it was with the apprehension of a novice thief that I turned the key in the lock. Closing his door with care, I leaned back against it.

The living room was larger than mine. And his bedroom, I noticed, was more spacious than mine. True enough, there was ample room for two people.

At this thought I brought up my head so smartly that it banged against the door. Swearing and going over to sit down on the sofa, I rubbed the back of my skull.

My eye was immediately drawn to a portfolio of drawings. Getting to my feet again, to open the portfolio flat on the ground, I located the triptych of Stairway C and a draft of what I took to be the next stage, the house. There were several sketches, studies of shapes and colors, tracings of various objects, the portrait Colin had shown me.

Next I discovered many drawings of myself, some of them dated a year back. This proved that since he first moved into the building, Colin had chosen me for a model. This was both disturbing and flattering. Studying each portrait in detail, I paid no further heed to the passing hours.

From time to time I fell upon a painting that was either openly abstract or a bit too figurative. It was as though he had trouble keeping a balance in his work. But there were also very beautiful things I admired at length. Quite clearly Colin possessed an artistic gift that was original, if still immature and sometimes awkward. But he was young. With age he would become assured.

Finally I found a sheet dated the twenty-fifth of the month and on which I read to my surprise, "A garden inclosed is my sister, my spouse; a spring shut up, a fountain sealed." Thinking back, I came to the conclusion that I was the one who had quoted this passage from the "Song of Songs." The most surprising part was that the page in question was free of all drawing. I imagined that he had been struck by the verse, that perhaps he wanted to try his hand at illustrating it.

Without thinking I turned over the paper. The blood suddenly took to pounding in my ears, for indeed there was something on the back. Me. Me!

Colin had chosen to represent me entirely nude, lounging against a wall. I felt myself blush violently, though persuaded that never had Colin seen me so. Perhaps without a shirt, but never naked! So here I had come upon the product of his fantasies, which had developed along with our evolving relationship.

But I couldn't understand what the *Song of Solomon* had to do with all this. Unless . . . what I had said in thinking of Rachel he had taken to himself. Viewed in that way, it became almost a declaration of love.

I kept on studying the drawing. On top of everything else, it had the nerve to be a good likeness. My chuckle of embarrassment turned into a gasp of terror as I heard the front door turning on its hinges. Since it was too late to do anything at all, I made every effort not to let my confusion show—no easy matter.

On seeing me sitting on the floor in front of his portfolio, Colin stopped dead.

"Hi!" I said jovially, in what I hoped was a normal tone of voice. "I couldn't bear to stay home alone, so I came up here to wait for you. Did your day go well? Mine didn't particularly—"

I broke off, afraid of overdoing it. What worried me was Colin's silence. He settled for slamming the door, a very bad sign.

"I was passing the time," I mumbled, making a clumsy effort to hide that particular drawing.

But apparently he had had plenty of time to see. As he came across the room I could tell that he was hurt and furious.

"Foster, you had no right!" he cried painfully, as though calling for help.

"I'm s-sorry," I stammered. "I meant no harm. I had no idea that—"

"Liar! I told you I didn't want to show them to you! You knew that perfectly well! And what're you doing here in my place, anyway? You're messing with my things!"

He punched me clumsily in the back, hitting hard, like a child on the verge of tears when a teasing adult has gone too far. I seized his wrist and held on as he tried to push me off.

"Come on, Colin! It's not serious!"

"Yes, it is! You've violated my secret garden!"

" 'A secret garden is my sister, my bride. A spring shut up, a fountain sealed.' "

He turned pale, mumbling something unintelligible.

"That's another translation of the *Song of Solomon,*" I said, all but laughing.

He tried to strike me with his free hand, which I seized. I must admit, I wasn't displeased to have the upper hand with Colin for once.

"Poor kid, they're picking on him!"

"Let me go! Ow!" As he collapsed against my shoulder with a sob, I could barely keep from smiling. He kept on struggling, with me still chiding him lightly, until he finally calmed down, more from exhaustion than good sense. It took him a moment to catch his breath before he could speak.

"You rat!"

"Okay for you, then. You're asking for more, kiddo?"

He broke away and began tidying up his portfolio all the while.

"You must have had a great old time," he suddenly blurted. "You'll be able to tell the whole thing to your girlfriend, and then you'll both make fun of me, won't you? In *her* bed."

"Oh, sure."

He began to cry.

"Colin! Stop it, you idiot!"

I drew him toward me, angry at myself. After staging a short-lived resistance, he let himself go and wept against my shoulder. After a few minutes he slipped his hand into mine with a deep breath that turned into a sigh.

"Mean . . ." he murmured.

"But I had no intention of being mean! To think that I came up here looking for comfort, yet I'm the one who's giving consolation."

He raised his damp face to look at me. "Comfort?"

"Oh, well, now I'm just fine, thanks."

He smiled, closing his eyes. "Foster . . ." he whispered, almost seductively.

"Yes?" I replied, unconsciously rubbing my cheek against his forehead.

"I'd really like you to kiss me."

I gave a start. How had I fallen for his little game? I drew back, much to Colin's surprise.

"Well, that's it for now. I've got things to do."

"Oh, really? What?"

Standing up, I absently brushed off my trousers.

"What?" he repeated under his breath.

Seeing the moment coming when he would begin to sulk again, I hastened to find some explanation.

"I've got stuff to write on Grindling Conrad, you know, the painter I've been dealing with."

I hoped he would swallow this most judiciously selected fib.

"Oh, then you'll have dinner with me?"

"No, I've just finished saying I haven't the time."

"That's exactly what I mean. I'll cook while you're working, and all you'll have to do is tuck your feet under the table."

"Uh . . . no. Oh, and anyway, I just remembered that I won't be in this evening."

" 'I won't be in this evening,' " he mimicked. " 'And I just remembered!' D'you take me for a fool?"

"No, for heaven's sake! Not in the least."

"You're going to her place again!" he burst out. "Damn her! Damn, lucky her!"

"But did I say any such thing? And first of all, what I do with my nights concerns no one but me."

"And is it good?"

"Is what good?"

"To have a woman."

"You've never tried it?"

"No."

"I suppose it's as good as having a man."

"You never tried?"

"A man? No. Never."

"Then you can't say it's just as good."

"Damn it, Colin. I said I *supposed* it is."

"Enough of your suppositions in that case. Why not make sure that it *is* just as good?"

"Colin! No! No way!"

I was astounded by his aplomb. In a way he had just asked me to spend the night with him.

In one great swoop I reached the door and opened it wide.

"You're always taking off," he protested.

"Maybe I am," I answered dryly. "But if you think you're going to jump me, you've got another think coming!"

"You're unfair! And you use words that hurt, that dirty everything!"

I started to shut the door behind me.

"I was speaking of love!" he cried out desperately.

I slammed the door. Not quickly enough, however, to avoid hearing Colin sob.

11. *A little girl with a watering can*

It was only on awakening from a night of tossing that I realized the phenomenal importance of my father's phone call. Sitting bolt upright in bed, I rapped my forehead with my knuckles.

I leapt out of bed, made a rapid calculation of the time difference, threw a bit of water on my face, picked up the receiver. At that precise moment the door bell rang. Who would dare?

Grumbling, I opened the door to find Colin Shepherd standing there with a frown. I regretted not having on a shirt.

"May we talk?" he asked gravely.

"If you like. But first I have to make an urgent phone call. I even invite you to listen in."

He sat himself down and crossed his arms. He did not look pleased, and I mean not the least bit pleased.

I dialed the number of the American Embassy in Switzerland and asked for Mr. Tuncurry. By great good fortune he was in.

"Mr. Tuncurry? Greetings, Tuncurry here."

"Well, hello, stranger. And to what do I owe the pleasure of *this* call, bane of my existence?"

"Dad, I'm going to tell you a story. Please don't interrupt until I'm finished."

"Foster, are you all right?"

"Everything's fine. Just listen, please." Then, before the wondering eyes of Colin Shepherd, I told him all: Mrs. Bernhardt's death, the various steps taken, the ashes, the Israeli Consulate, everything. With the exception of Rachel.

"Do you see?" I concluded. "That woman had one last

172

wish, and it's up to me to do everything to carry it out. Dad, are you still there?''

"But what can I do?''

"The idiots here will never give way, not even if you intervene. But . . . perhaps you're in good standing with the Israeli diplomats in Switzerland.''

"So I am, but . . .''

"It's simple, Dad. All we have to do is get the urn as far as Switzerland, then set off again with a legal authorization that you'll have obtained.''

"Oh, is that so? It's all very simple! And you think anyone at all can wander about, just like that, on a plane, with somebody's ashes?''

"But, Dad, there's no problem for *you.* ''

"Just what are you implying?''

"Well, I was thinking of the diplomatic pouch.''

A brief silence settled over the phone line. Then suddenly a strange, strident sound reached me. I had to bow to the facts: My father was choking with laughter.

"That's the limit!'' he finally responded. "Something really amusing has finally happened to me in this benighted profession!''

"I'm delighted that you find all this hilarious, father mine, but do you agree to it?''

"Agree? I find it so amusing that I couldn't possibly refuse.''

I drew a sigh of relief.

"So you'll take care of it? And when you leave for Switzerland after your visit here, I'll go along with you, okay?''

"Oh, whatever you like.'' And he began to laugh again. "You know, Foster, there are moments when I actually find you rewarding as a son.''

"The feeling's mutual, Pop.''

"Listen, I've got to hang up now. I'm lunching with the French ambassador. He's a good friend, and believe you me, he's going to have one big laugh when he hears what the diplomatic pouch is used for these days.''

"Well, if it provokes ambassadorial laughter, I've done my bit for global solidarity.''

"My love to you, wretched son, and see you soon.''

"Fare thee well, ignominious father.''

I put down the receiver and rubbed my hands together. "There, that does it," I crowed. "This time I'm nearing success."

I turned to Colin, whose expression clearly indicated that he considered me completely off my rocker.

"It's really the only answer," I said by way of excuse. "I've tried all the others."

I suggested making some coffee, to give him time to recover. Apparently he was stunned to the point of forgetting why he had come. He followed me into the kitchen.

"Foster . . . so this was the reason for all that mystery?"

"Seems ridiculous, doesn't it? You can understand that I didn't want to talk about it."

"It's not ridiculous."

"Laughable, in that case."

"Real courage is made of laughable actions."

"A thought from Mao?" I couldn't help teasing a bit.

"No, it's mine."

"That's almost as good."

"So many things about you simply escape me."

"And a good thing too! At least you can have the pleasure of discovery."

"What bothers me is that I was very angry when I came in here, and I'm not at all anymore."

"I wouldn't complain about it. But what was the cause of your anger?"

"Mainly that you don't give a shit about me! You play with me. And you keep hurting me a bit more by the moment."

I bit my lip, making an impatient gesture that wound up as a violent meeting of my elbow and the cupboard door. I swore and rubbed the elbow. What the devil had I done to deserve this pastime of banging into everything within reach?

"Foster . . ."

I had the instant impression that Colin was about to ask me something very, very unpleasant. Instinctively I stiffened, on the defensive.

"Foster," he repeated, visibly embarrassed.

"So now you're scared to talk to me?"

"Beatrice lives with Virgil, Sharon with Bruce," he began oddly, "and we—"

"What's this we?"

"My place is large, certainly more spacious than yours. . ."

I didn't answer but concentrated on looking him in the eye as coldly as possible.

"And then . . . it's all the same to me if you have your girl-friends. Sure, I'm jealous, but I make no demands. All I'd like is for you to live with me. I know that in the long run I'd win out."

"Win out? But what do you mean by that?"

"That a time will come when you'll accept yourself as you are."

"And what am I?"

"A man . . . who loves another man." He blushed, almost as disturbed as I was. "And what the hell," he blurted. "I love you, and I don't give a damn about the rest of it."

"I don't suppose you're expecting an immediate reply?"

"You need time to think it over?"

"At the very least."

"Well, that means you're not saying no!" He beamed with pleasure.

"Wait a moment! I didn't say yes, either," I protested.

"Doesn't matter. Maybe is often yes."

"And sometimes no, baby face."

"I thought you were going to beat me up, and here you are calling me pet names."

"It was intended ironically," I retorted, chiding myself.

"No matter, ironic or no, I was expecting the worst."

We went back to the living room with the coffee. After a long pause Colin spoke up.

"I think I began to love you the day you told me you detested green peas. Remember?"

"Yes, in the supermarket."

"Right. And then, not too long ago, Beatrice told me that you had decided to help me while the others at the time weren't at all in favor of it. You see, Foster, you were already interested in me too."

"That's largely because I don't like running into people in the stairway who're streaming blood."

"Sure, sure . . . doesn't change a thing. Admit that you're unable to have a lasting love relationship with a woman."

"That I've never denied. But it doesn't prove a thing, unless it's that I have a lousy personality."

He smiled, stretching. "I could easily go for a bit of food. How about some toast?"

"If you like."

I went to put together a slightly more filling breakfast, corn flakes for me, leaving the toast to Colin. After briefly contemplating the slices of bread, he pushed them toward me. I raised a questioning eyebrow.

"Could you butter them for me?" he asked.

"You can't do it yourself?"

"Sure, but I'd like you to."

"What's this all about?"

"Nothing. I'd simply like you to do it."

I gave up trying to understand and undertook to spread the butter. I had scarcely begun when he stopped me.

"Thanks, that'll do. I know what I wanted to know."

"But?" I said, rather puzzled. "Know what, first of all? What is this scheme?"

"Just a while ago you'd have hurled the plate in my face. In any case, you wouldn't have done what I asked, right?"

"And exactly what do you deduce from that?"

"That you've decided to trust others. That's not bad for starters. Also, that you're ready to accede to my wishes, whatever they might be, without immediately putting up opposition. And that's even better."

"And you, how about going to get my shirt in the bedroom?"

"Out of the question."

"Hey, that's not fair! If I do something for you, you've got to do the same for me."

"That's an altogether democratic point of view, but, you see, I have full intentions of being a despot."

He bit into a piece of toast to hide the trace of a smile, but the gleam in his eyes left no room for doubt: He was making fun of me.

"Idiot," I grumbled.

I shivered. And went to get the shirt myself.

"Are you taking me to Israel, Foster?"

"No. It's my problem. I want to be alone there."

He seemed disappointed.

"I promise to write," I added. "And, anyway, I won't be gone for long. Come to think of it, I'll give you my answer in the letter I'll send you. You can consider that my pause for reflection. What do you think?''

"I'll go along with that.''

"And when my father comes, I'll have you meet him.''

"Do you think that's wise?''

"No, but my father's far from wise himself, so it cancels out. Besides, I'm curious to see his reaction.''

"You want me as a guinea pig for your experiments?''

"Hell, no. I just want to see what he'll say about you.''

With a rub of his eyes Colin gave a deep yawn. "Damn, damn, damn . . . gotta go off to work.''

"Such enthusiasm!''

"That's it, keep right on making fun of me.'' He slowly got to his feet and moved toward the door. "See you soon.''

On the dot of eleven-thirty I had a surprise visit from Vanessa and Grindling.

"Hi, there,'' said Vanessa. "We've come to ask you out for lunch.''

"Today? Just like that?''

"Exactly,'' she replied. "And you're even going to spend part of the afternoon in our worthy company.''

"Oh, am I?'' I replied with some amusement.

"Yessir. There's something we want to show you at the Met. The National Art Gallery has loaned New York a painting or two.''

"And that's where you're taking me?''

"That's where. And to be quite frank, we have a little idea in mind.''

I had no chance to learn more, for they dragged me off then and there.

Our meal together was most pleasant. Among other things, I learned that Vanessa and Grindling had scarcely spent a moment apart since I had introduced them.

"Poor Foster, he'll be jealous,'' Vanessa mocked.

"Not I,'' I retorted. "You know me and little Polish immigrants.''

"Hey, hey! See the way he talks to me, Grindling?''

Grindling Conrad smiled enigmatically but said nothing. Over dessert he finally spoke up and asked whether I felt altogether healthy again.

"I'm no longer sick, at any rate."

"You know, I've always felt that you were suffering in the mind more than the body. Now you look happy, recovered."

I made do with putting two lumps of sugar in my coffee.

"Aren't you happy?" he persisted.

"Sure. Actually my fault was in reacting to things with the intellect only. But I was terribly bruised in body. Only now have I learned to respond with gut feelings. Strange, isn't it?"

"Salutary, it would appear."

"Yes, that's the word."

"That will add poignancy to the ensuing events," he added with a wink toward Vanessa.

"And just what is that supposed to mean?" I asked, stirring my decaf.

"You'll see, my friend," she replied, pointing a finger at me.

What I saw, as it turned out, was the show sent up from Washington by the National Art Gallery. We had wandered through the first few rooms at the Met before I realized that I was being led toward a very precise destination.

"Here we are," said Grindling, suddenly holding me by the arm. "We'll leave you here with the young lady."

Pointing me toward a painting, he went off with Vanessa. "We'll be back," he said across his shoulder.

Somewhat surprised, I watched them disappear before turning to the young lady in question.

I scarcely wanted to keep my eyes open. But who could resist? Sweetness, tenderness, the sun of her smile illuminated the whole of the green-and-ochre canvas. On her fragile blond hair, the hue of ripe wheat, perched a bright red butterfly. Was it a mischievous hand or a gust of wind that had placed there this vermillion bow, ready to take flight? She was looking at someone or something she must have loved. The flowers in her left hand seemed to be withering, and the watering can would do nothing to save them.

I returned her smile with a nod. "Hello. Lovely day, isn't it?" Somewhat nippy, perhaps. But never mind, her royal-blue velvet dress was warm enough with its springlike lace and white buttons.

Suddenly my cheeks were burning. Was I intimidated? No, I

was ashamed. My impure eyes must be sullying so much innocence. My heart caught fire. I was in love.

"Do you suppose he's been standing there for a full forty-five minutes?" said a voice at my elbow.

"So it would seem," said another voice.

With great difficulty I tore myself away from the light to find myself blinded and dazed. For a moment I could distinguish nothing beyond a gray haze. Ultimately two shapes emerged and took on color.

"Were you enjoying yourself, Foster?" Vanessa asked.

"Yes, thanks. I've always had a way with little girls. Like Anita. Remember?"

"Yeah, the impossible brat at the opening."

Grindling was dividing his attention between me and the Renoir. "Feelings? Reactions?" he remarked.

"Impossible to describe. . . . I'll simply say warmth and clarity. Is that an adequate response?"

"Conclusive, then?"

"Unexpected. And unsought."

The three of us went off together before separating. Grindling and Vanessa leaned against one another as they walked arm in arm. I was alone. But the air was balmy, and at last I no longer felt cold.

Toward late afternoon the telephone rang. Again I thought sadly of that mechanical wonder called the answering machine, which, no doubt, I'll never buy. It was Florence Fairchild. I greeted her with some reserve.

"Foster, you seem a bit distant," she eventually remarked. "Is there something wrong?"

"Well, look, Florence, this is a bit difficult. I'm fond enough of you to owe you the truth and yet to fear hurting you. A most embarrassing situation, isn't it?"

"You give me pause. Explain away. I'm all ears."

"Here it is. To be absolutely honest, I don't love you. I mean, I'm not in love with you. . . ."

"And so?"

"That doesn't seem to arouse any great reaction?"

"To tell the truth, it doesn't."

"In a way I'm relieved. Though a bit annoyed."

"You'd rather I were suffering?"

"God, no! To the great good fortune of others as well as myself, I've lost the habit of that pastime."

"If I understand correctly, we can still be good friends?"

"I certainly hope so."

"In that case, may I ask you one small question, in the most friendly fashion?"

"You bet. Go ahead."

"You're in love with someone else?"

Pausing, I smiled. "As a matter of fact, I don't know," I admitted.

"That young woman at the opening?"

"Who? Oh, the one with the feathers? No, not her. Anyway, since then she's been living with Grindling Conrad."

"You don't mean it!"

I considered it unnecessary to say right out that the object of my uneasiness was my upstairs neighbor. There's such a thing as pride. But since that notion turned me against my own cowardice, I forced myself to answer her frankly.

"Do you remember when we passed a young man on the stairs in my building? Blond, halfway between Botticelli's *Spring* and Renoir's little girls?"

"Yes, perfectly. And so?"

"He's the one I mean."

"Beg your pardon?" She paused for what seemed a lifetime. "Foster, are you pulling my leg?"

"Does it shock you? I'm not surprised. You and your middle-class morality!"

"Foster!"

"Have I shrunk in your esteem, perhaps because I might choose a man over Florence Fairchild?"

"Did I say that?"

"No, I'm the one who's saying it. A month ago I'd have murdered anyone who dared suggest such a thing. I never realized anybody could change so fundamentally in the space of a month. I thought one couldn't evolve at all once past a certain age. As you see, I was mistaken. If you only knew how strongly I feel that my life was on the wrong course."

"Not insofar as Grindling Conrad is concerned, that I assure you!"

"Well, at least there's that much to say for it. After all, I've always existed for art alone. It's only now that I realize—rather painfully, in fact—that there's more than art.''

"Love?" she asked.

"Yes but not only that. Or rather, love taken in its larger sense. God, life, death, friendship, emotions. I was somewhat of a stranger to all that. As though you were talking to me about bacteria. I know they exist, but aside from that . . . And then, too, I'd forged such fine armor of indifference for myself. With helmet on head, entirely constructed of meanness. Do you know anything about the fear of suffering?''

"Not really."

"Well, you're lucky. Because it's terrifying. It's the most direct route to emptiness and destruction. I know, I've been there. Hurting is merely the other side of pleasure. If one is never hurt . . . .''

"One is never happy?"

"Exactly. Ah! It's great to be intelligent, but there are days when I'd rather be a dope. Just the least bit, in order to see if happiness is worth the effort we poor mortals expend on it.''

"And you believe that to be stupid automatically implies being happy?''

"I've no idea. But since intelligence means unhappiness, I must conclude that the opposite is true as well.''

"Then I must be stupid."

"So much the better for you!"

She laughed, then turned serious again. "In ten minutes you've said more to me than in a whole evening. At last I'm beginning to get a clear picture of what you are.''

"Better late than never. And better never than too late.''

"Why?"

"Because there are no regrets."

"That's happened to you?"

"Yes, but don't ask me further. Remember the line from Shelley? 'Inheritor of more than earth can give'?''

"That's pertinent?"

"Yes and no. Even if it weren't, it's a lovely line.''

"Have you any more like that in your pocket?"

"Oh, lots! 'Once upon a time, a very long time ago, about last Friday, Winnie the Pooh lived in a forest all by himself under the name of Sanders.' So quoth A. A. Milne.''

Florence laughed. "That certainly doesn't give an impression of suitable gravity."

"Perhaps, but I know many stories of that sort by heart. I recited them to myself so often when I was a kid."

"The great Foster Tuncurry, specialist in Hieronymus Bosch and Winnie the Pooh."

"The two go rather well together, I feel."

We kept on chattering this way for a good twenty minutes. I told her I was leaving for Switzerland and Israel without saying exactly why, of course. We decided to see one another again on my return. As friends.

Time having the fearsome habit of rushing on and rarely pausing, we had already come around again to the day of our monthly dinner. But everything had changed. First of all, we had increased by two. Also, our days of confirmed bachelorhood were long gone.

To me Bruce's apartment seemed too small. The music was drowned out by the sound of our voices, and I missed my one-to-one with Beatrice in front of the speakers. Poor Ravel had fallen from favor. I was beginning to sink into melancholy and into my glass of bourbon when Bruce came to sit down beside me.

"Well, there, old buddy, you're not very talkative tonight," he said with a slap on my thigh.

I gave the excuse of slight weariness. And then he suddenly leaned toward me, almost resting his head against my shoulder.

"Foster, I wanted to say . . ." He spoke under his breath.

I waited anxiously for him to finish the sentence.

"Thanks," he whispered very softly. Then he sprang up and walked across the room. Naturally I could feel the warmth rise to my cheeks, due to the alcohol and the overheated room. I surprised myself by stroking the cat, who seemed equally surprised, though elated. Anita sat down right beside me, her hand on my arm.

"I played all afternoon long," she said.

I did my best to seem interested.

"It's not fair, because Bruce can play all the time if he wants to," she went on.

"Oh, really?"

"Yes. He took me along with him, so I know."

I felt some apprehension. Would Bruce have had the temerity to take Anita to the clinic? "You went to see the children, uh . . . in the big house?" I asked.

"Yes. And they sure are lucky."

"Is that so? Why?"

"Well, look . . . they get to play all day long."

Refraining from comment, I listened to Anita's saga in detail. She made no mention of anything strange. Except when she remembered that there was a little boy called Paul, and he wasn't playing but only sitting in a corner by himself.

"If you ask me," she said, resting her head against me, "he must have been sulking."

For dinner, by sheer luck—or perhaps it wasn't—I found myself on the sofa, with Colin sitting between me and Bruce. Colin, who had not yet said a word to me all evening, smiled timidly but firmly contrived to avoid catching my eye.

"Is there some problem?" I asked, somewhat anxiously.

"No, no. I'm simply in training."

"What the hell for?"

"To look as though I weren't interested in you. For when your father comes."

I snickered at his stupidity. "But, look, Colin, that's the very best way to show that you are interested in me. At any rate, if I want you to meet my father, it's precisely to see his reaction to us as a couple. At least as a potential couple."

"And if he doesn't like it?"

"Then what on earth could he do about it? Disinherit me for the three hundred and fiftieth time? No. And anyway, I know him. I'm almost sure you'll like him. He's a special case, my dear father. And he still cuts a fine figure for a man of his age."

"What if I turn out to like him better than you?"

"My mother wouldn't be overjoyed, I guess."

"It never occurred to me that you had a mother."

"Whaddya think—I was hatched?" He laughed. And I went on. "Do you know we've never spoken about *your* parents?"

"Let 'em croak!"

"Why?"

"I detest them, and God knows they're the ones who taught me to feel that way. That's actually all I ever got from them, hatred. Shame, despair. I got out of there. As quickly and as far as possible. But I don't want to go on about it. I've put them out of mind. I want so badly to be happy."

I passed him the platter of fried shrimp quite noncommittally, and he thanked me . . . noncommittally.

"Happy," I repeated, half aloud. Hearing me, he turned my way. "It's one of those idiotic words whose real meaning we can never know for sure," I added.

"What makes you say that?"

"Because the meaning of the word is purely relative."

"Yes. It all depends on the individual."

"Yes, but not only that. It can also depend on the events, the situations."

"Look here, guys!" Bruce Conway was leaning across the table. "All philosophy is strictly forbidden in this honorable establishment. Do be so kind as to check it at the door."

The next day my father showed up around seven in the evening. Needless to say, he had not told me when to expect him. Scanning the room critically, he frowned.

"I would never get used to these miserable digs," he commented.

"I intend to move out," I replied. "I'm thinking of going to the apartment just upstairs."

Taking Colin's keys, I drew my father along with me. "Come on, we'll go up. You'll be able to judge for yourself."

His enthusiasm for climbing yet another flight was not overwhelming. "But, son, I just got here!" I scoffed at him as I opened Colin's door.

The latter, at work on a drawing, looked up with surprise. His astonishment turned to panic when he caught sight of my father.

"See, Dad," I remarked, "there's much more space here."

Colin awkwardly wiped his fingers blackened by charcoal.

"I'd like you to meet Colin Shepherd, Dad. Colin, this is my father."

They exchanged greetings. My father looked Colin over quickly and attentively, then turned back to me.

"And if you move in here," he asked, "will you keep all the furniture?"

"Yes, I suppose so."

It was not hard to detect an undercurrent to his question.

"There are some pretty things here," he said, taking a seat.

Reacting at last, Colin managed to articulate a few words.

"Would you like a drink, Mr. Tuncurry?"

"Excellent idea. And do call me Nigel. In our family we've always had the ridiculous habit of using first names. So I'll have a whiskey in a tall glass."

As Colin handed it to him, my father caught him by the arm. "Young man, if I ask for a tall glass, it's that I also want a tall whiskey." And he tipped up the bottle above his glass.

"There, that's more like it."

Increasingly disconcerted, Colin sat down beside me without a thought of offering me anything at all.

"I could use a bit of sherry," I said.

Startled, he got to his feet again. "Oh, sorry."

My father followed each of his movements with a persistence that would have bothered most people. Once Colin was seated again, he began to query him.

"And what do you do, young man?"

Colin put down his glass with a trembling hand. "I'm a fashion designer, sir."

"Oh, are you? Does it pay well?"

"Uh, yes, sir. Rather well."

"Can you adequately take on the support of another person in that case?"

"Yes," mumbled Colin, swallowing painfully.

"Very good. You know that my son is an impossible person?"

"I'd noticed as much. But perhaps it's just a question of knowing how to handle him."

Then Colin blushed at his own effrontery. He made a move to rise, saying something about having forgotten the crackers. I firmly grabbed his arm and made him sit still. He shot me a glance out of the corner of his eye, not daring to disobey. I let my hand linger briefly on his wrist just to be sure my father noticed. Then I stood up myself and went to fetch the appetizers.

"It appears you know the place well, my son."

"True, very well," I threw back. "Colin and I are old friends." When I returned to the living room with the plate, my father had more sallies in store for me.

"Your mother urged me to question you discreetly about any girlfriends you might be serious about? What shall I tell her?"

"Nothing, since I'll be seeing her myself in a few days' time."

I wondered whether this game of verbal hide-and-seek would go on for long.

My father turned to Colin. "Is the fashion world fun?" he asked abruptly.

"Not too much. But it's not boring. I can work a lot at home."

"What do you feel is Foster's most significant virtue, if indeed he has one?"

Colin was nonplussed. "His greatest virtue is his worst fault," he replied.

"And just what is that?" I asked with some surprise.

"Your intelligence."

My father laughed. "Very good, very good. I share your view. Even when Foster was a child, I couldn't bear his intelligence, while at the same time I had to admire it. They're exasperating, the overly gifted."

"I don't feel overly gifted, Dad. My knowledge is no broader than anyone else's. The difference is simply that it isn't made up of the same elements. It's not that I know *more,* I know *other things.*"

"Hmm . . . and according to you, Foster, what is your friend's greatest virtue?"

Colin turned to me, waiting for the answer to my father's unfair question.

"His patience," I replied.

"And his worst fault?"

"He's always right. And that's unbearable!"

"I'd be curious to observe your mother in the position you've put me in," said my father with a smile.

"Oh, but I'd never have placed her in this situation."

"Is this preferential treatment? Still being a pain in the ass for me?"

"Is that the language of diplomacy?"

"Is this the way to treat a poor defenseless father?"

Colin sank into his corner of the sofa, seared by the turn of events.

"You've always behaved in the most fucking awful way with me!" my father went on.

"Such language! Are you going to disinherit me?"

"I decided on that the moment I laid eyes on your fashion designer. And all because you had the nerve to choose someone young, handsome, rich, and charming. Since I can't detest him, I naturally have to take it out on you, unworthy son!"

"Following your usual bent, scourge of the young!"

"Intellectual! Decadent!"

"Diplomat!"

"Ah, now there you've gone too far!" he protested.

And we both roared with laughter, to the consternation of Colin Shepherd, who couldn't understand any of it.

"You really love my son?" my father asked him intently.

Colin turned scarlet, which didn't escape my father, who smiled at him benevolently.

"Yes," Colin answered, quickly attempting to hide his confusion by gulping down his sherry.

"A curious notion, to tell the truth."

"Perhaps," said Colin, his cheeks still aflame.

"And you believe my son loves you?" he persisted, somewhat wickedly.

"Yes. But he's not so sure."

"Would you like a bit of advice, young man?"

"No. But that won't prevent you from giving it."

"Now how about that? He does have assurance, after all."

"He may not look it," I put in, "but he's a granite wall. At any rate, I'm dying to hear what sort of advice you might have to offer."

"This will come as a surprise to you. Young man," he went on, turning to Colin, "take hold."

"Just what does that mean?" Colin asked.

"That, when all is said and done, my son is worth the pains we give ourselves on his behalf."

For the moment it was my turn to be rendered speechless. Flattered as well.

"You're also aware that Foster is quite mad?"

"Yes, absolutely," Colin said. "But at times there can be gentle madness, very gentle."

Far from being frightened, Colin was clearly beginning to appreciate the singular personality, to say the least, of Mr. Tuncurry Senior.

"There's nothing you can teach Colin, Dad. He knows more than you about my case."

"Is that so? He is aware that nowadays you're into transporting cadavers?"

"They happen to be ashes," I retorted. "And, anyway, it is *you* who will be carrying them in your own little suitcase."

His face lit up. "The French ambassador doubled over when I told him the story. He wants, at all costs, to meet you when we get to Berne."

"So I'll have my permission?"

"Oh, no problem."

"Perfect," I said with satisfaction.

So I had won out. A heavy weight was suddenly lifted from my chest. I felt as though I could breathe freely again.

Colin was watching me, a faint smile on his lips. I caught his eye.

"Tuncurry Inc., Bodies by Air!" my father joked. "Who knows? Maybe you've fallen into the business of the future."

"Undertaking?"

"Yes, they'll always be needed. Particularly these days."

"Ah, yes," I said with a chuckle, "there's nothing but misery, misery all around."

Since my father had decided to ask us out to dinner, it was twelve-thirty by the time I dropped him off at his hotel. I pushed the formalities to the point of accompanying him into the lobby while Colin kept the cab. Taking out his key, he made one last remark in his most severe tone of voice.

"He's charming, that young man."

And with that he got into the elevator, allowing me no chance to reply.

We got back to Stairway C feeling a bit squiffed. Colin stopped off at my place for a cup of tea, which he deemed well earned. Eyes half-closed, he collapsed onto my sofa. By the time I returned with my tray, he had taken off his jacket and unbuttoned his shirt. I gazed at him a moment. He seemed asleep, his face relaxed, with a self-assured expression. When I struck two spoons together, he opened his eyes. After a long pause I opened the conversation.

"You know, there's a terrific exhibit going on now at the Met. On loan from the National Gallery."

"Oh? Is it interesting?"

"Not all of it, of course." I took a few sips of tea before I could go on. "However, there is this . . . this Renoir."

"Oh, yeah, *Little Girl with a Watering Can?*"

"So you know all about the exhibition?"

"No, but I know the painting belongs to the National. So you didn't like it?"

"That's just it, I did. But it bothers me some."

"How's that?"

"I scorned that painting for ten years of my life. I never would have dreamt that I could love two opposite things at once."

"Because opposition is only in appearances. But what was the basic nature of those things?"

I had to laugh. He wasn't altogether wrong.

"I believe that fundamentally no two real opposites exist," he went on. "Except in the case of lovers who repel each other. But, after all, you only have to turn one of them around for them to attract one another."

"And what do you make of love and hatred?"

He paused to think it over. "This is difficult, but since you asked . . . Love being Absolute, meaning God, Hatred is also Absolute, meaning . . . God."

"That's not very cheerful."

"But look how weighed down man is by original sin. Our feelings aren't exactly negligible, after all."

"Sure they are. Negligible. Contemptible."

"Oh, come on. . . . Sometimes they lead us to the light."

"Light is an optical illusion. All you have to do is cut off the electricity to convince yourself of that."

"That's absurd! In any case, darkness exists only because of light."

"Which simply goes to prove that opposition does exist."

"No. You simply have the same problem ad infinitum."

"Infinity, which exists only in relation to the finite, et cetera, et cetera. . . . All I know is that I exist, and that *Little Girl with a Watering Can* exists too. I somehow cannot take that in."

When Colin left that night, he asked me to take him to see the painting. I first hesitated, before refusing. But I advised him to go if he wanted to.

Then I asked him a great favor. I begged him not to try to see me before my departure for Switzerland. Though it cost him dearly, he agreed. With a renewed promise to write, I thanked him.

On the doorstep we shook hands.

12. *Here I am*

The heat in the Ben Gurion Airport was intense, but I bore up under all of it, including the crowds. I left that most ordinary of places by taxi, the urn in my knapsack resting on my knees.

My first act on reaching the hotel was to find a postcard. On it I wrote ''Here I am'' and sent it off to the Emigration Service of the Israeli Consulate in New York. Nobody back there would be able to make a particle of sense out of it, but a promise is a promise.

I still had to write Colin. Too cowardly to be completely open, I settled for a quotation, for which L. Frank Baum would surely forgive me.

> ''All the same,'' said the Scarecrow, ''I'll ask for brains instead of a heart; for a fool would not know what to do with a heart if he had one.''
>
> ''I shall take the heart,'' returned the Tin Woodsman, ''for brains do not make one happy, and happiness is the best thing in the world.''

It was hot in Jerusalem, too, when I reached it by a rental car. With the help of my guidebook I set off in search of the Jewish cemeteries. Taking the road toward Gethsemane, I climbed for almost a mile through olive groves.

I was reluctant to enter this region of disorder, midway between a marble quarry and an archaeological excavation. But then my determination revived, and I pushed on into the deserted area.

A swirl of wind raised the dust. For a moment or two I sat in the shade of a huge white tomb and gazed out over Jerusalem.

I took the urn, the photograph of Rachel, and the bracelet out of my bag. I picked up a stone and patiently, methodically, I broke the seals on the urn. Without any feeling of embarrassment or apprehension I took off the lid, and taking care not to look inside, I shook out the ashes into the wind. For a moment they whirled around, then scattered, then came together again and rose to the sky.

Next I burned the photograph.

Taking up the stone, I smashed the funerary urn and pounded the bracelet. Its charms tinkled for the last time.

I scattered everything that remained—unrecognizable scraps.

Facing the sun, I took a few steps forward. Its light did not dazzle me. The heat was not uncomfortable. The wind failed to make me blink.

In the distance, olive trees were stirring in a breeze.